The Courage to Grieve

The Courage to Grieve

by Judy Tatelbaum

PERENNIAL LIBRARY

Harper & Row, Publishers, New York
Grand Rapids, Philadelphia, St. Louis, San Francisco
London, Singapore, Sydney, Tokyo, Toronto

A hardcover edition of this book is published by Lippincott & Crowell, Publishers, Inc.

Designer: Vikki Sheatsley

Library of Congress Cataloging in Publication Data

Tatelbaum, Judy.
  The courage to grieve.

  Bibliograpy: p.
  Includes index.
  1. Grief. I. Title.
BF575.G7T38 1984   155.9′37   84-47621
ISBN 0-06-091185-9 (pbk.)

99 00 01   RRD 40 39 38 37 36 35 34 33 32

This book is dedicated to

David Henry Tatelbaum (1935–1956) . . . brother

Lorraine Barnet (1936–1965) . . . friend

Melvin Boigon, M.D. (1920–1969) . . . wise counselor

Kit Parker . . . for his love and support

Esther Beckler Tatelbaum and Abraham Tatelbaum, M.D. . . .
  for giving me life and a desire to live a life of meaning

Jim Simkin . . . for helping me find the courage to transform
  my life

Every human being with whom I have shared an intimate moment
  . . . for those are the richest moments I have known.

Contents

PART FOUR

Grief Resolution

PART FIVE

Self-Help

Acknowledgments

While I am solely responsible for the ideas presented in this book, I am grateful to my many friends and clients who shared themselves, their feelings, and their grief with me. I am honored by our intimacy. Although I have not used any of my clients' real names, I hope they will recognize themselves and their contributions to this book. I am blessed with extraordinary friends, many of whom contributed to this book. Nancy Rushmer provoked me to write in the first place because of her courage in grieving. Tom Berman gave me a magnificent example of courage in his dealings with cancer. Ev and Al Parker gave me love and the encouragement to be creative. Stephanie Matthews-Simonton appeared in my life and helped me at crucial points in the writing and publication process. Several friends helped me and stimulated my ideas because of their reading of the manuscript, especially Zoe Snyder, Nancy Joeckel, Hanna Fox, Toni Flint, Marta Bennett, and Lyn Friedman, who also typed the manuscript expertly. Bob Mirandon provided valuable editorial assistance. My special gratitude to my agent, Jed Mattes, and to my editor at Lippincott & Crowell, Lawrence Peel Ashmead, for their faith in me and my book.

The Courage
to Grieve

Prologue

Your joy is your sorrow unmasked.
And the selfsame well from which
your laughter rises was oftentimes
filled with your tears.
—KAHLIL GIBRAN, The Prophet

On March 17, 1956, my brother, David, age twenty, was killed in an automobile accident. I was seventeen, a senior in high school then. I couldn't face the reality. I pretended that his death was a lie and that the policeman who informed us had made a mistake. I imagined David would reappear at any moment and prove me right.

As time went on, and David didn't reappear, I felt an overwhelming sense of loss. I missed him terribly. I agonized about why I did not die instead of David. I felt helpless, knowing how much my parents must be suffering. I did not know what to do for them or say to them. I envied intact families, now that we were three instead of four. I didn't want to be an only child. I was afraid of the dark that reminded me of death. David was in all my dreams. These dreams of reunion made me happy and at the same time made me want to die to be with him again. My sense of loss was revived each morning, when I realized being with David was only a dream.

Although seeing David's body at the funeral forced me to acknowledge the truth of his death, it still took me years to accept it. My feelings of loss were so intense and overwhelming that periodically I would retreat into my denial of his death. My grief came and went, over and over again. I hated my sorrow and yet felt guilty when I forgot about it.

I was angry at the reckless driver who caused the accident and at God for letting such a vital young man die. I asked the question "Why?" over and over again. People kept saying David's death was "God's will." What kind of God would will David dead? God looked wrathful and frightening to me. I wondered if I was a fool to believe in God at all.

My lack of a belief system made my grief more painful. For years a sense of meaninglessness pervaded my life. I went through the motions of living: school, dating, working as a social worker, marriage, divorce, and other new experiences. I saw life as an empty struggle, hard work without much reward. I thought a lot about dying. I wrote poetry and short stories about my hopelessness. I was treading water, getting through somehow, but certainly not relishing my life. I felt guilty to be alive when David was not, and I missed him still.

I searched for a way to accept death. I longed to find meaning in life and death. Few people would even talk with me about death and loss. My graduate training in social work at Simmons College in Boston confirmed how profound the trauma of loss is for people, but it did not help me resolve my sorrow. I wasted three years in therapy with a psychiatrist who could not face grief and death himself and who kept telling me to grow up. I felt myself questing alone, searching out answers through philosophers and gingerly exploring some religions. In 1966 I went to another psychiatrist in New York, Mel Boigon, a wise and loving man who helped me face my grief and work through more of it. Then Mel died unexpectedly at the age of forty-eight. It was a terrible loss but I faced it squarely. I wanted to show Mel that I could, to testify to his helping me. Now, at last, I discovered my strength and ability to face death.

I did not completely finish with my brother's death until 1970, when I participated in a professional training workshop with Jim Simkin, Ph.D., the renowned Gestalt therapist. Through working on an angry dream, I discovered my unfinished business with David—my secret anger at him for dying, anger which was unacceptable to me. At last I was able to say good-bye to David and, I realized afterward, to years of depression as well. This personal experience of mine is detailed in chapter 12.

The profundity of that experience with Gestalt therapy led me to give up being a traditional psychotherapist and to train with Jim in 1972. Gestalt therapy enabled me to not only finish grieving but also to come alive at last and find real joy in living.

This psychological healing led to my opening up to the spiritual dimension of life. I felt enormous gratitude to God or the Universe for helping me find my way at last. I was interested in death in a new way. My curiosity grew as I studied meditation and read metaphysical books that described life after death and reincarnation. I was particularly moved by the Edgar Cayce material; by Ruth Montgomery's books, *Here and Hereafter, The Search for Truth,* and *A World Beyond;* and by Jess Stearn's book, *The Search for a Soul: Taylor Caldwell's Psychic Lives.*

At the same time, in examining my recurrent dream about my brother, I realized that for almost twenty years David had been telling me in dreams that he lived somewhere else, a place where I cannot go—yet. With my analytic background and skepticism, it took me twenty years to accept a message of life after death.

Moving confirmation of my own beliefs came in 1976 when I attended a conference on death and dying in Berkeley, California, organized by John F. Kennedy University. Doctors Elisabeth Kübler-Ross, Raymond Moody, Ernest Pecci, and Charles Garfield talked about their experiences working with the dying, and all publicly shared their beliefs in life after death and reincarnation with an audience of one thousand.

On September 9, 1978, my friend Nancy Rushmer's eighteen-year-old daughter, Teri, died with three other young people in the crash of a light plane. Nancy, believing that Teri's soul lived on, coped with her grief with a kind of courage I had never seen before. That Nancy found her spiritual beliefs such a source of strength contrasted with my own bitter experience with David's death. I wanted to write about that. Instead I found pouring out of me a book on grief and how to cope with it, seeing spirituality as one of many supports that enable people to grieve courageously and survive.

It seems no accident that I began to write this book around my dreaded fortieth birthday. I am bewildered to be forty so soon. Whatever happened to thirty and twenty? Time is passing quickly. I am closer to the end of my life than I would like to be. At twenty I disliked the sense that life felt endless, and I liked the idea that I had plenty of time. Now I no longer feel that I have plenty of time. I want to act now, before it is too late, and that certainly is a message of this book.

As I began writing, a powerful awareness hit me that my whole life has been geared to writing precisely this book about grief. I have always been conscious of grief and curious about death. For years, especially after I finished my own personal grieving, much of the therapy I have done has been related to grief. I have spent most of my life learning to be unafraid of loss and death. I have a wealth of experience to share, and I want to help others be unafraid and courageous too.

Only after I had written many pages did I remember that when my brother died the memorial I most wanted to give him then was to write a book to dedicate to him. How amazing and how fitting that I am dedicating this book on grief to David, twenty-four years later! I want this to be a book of hope and understanding that helps others to grieve fully, to finish with their grief more quickly than I did, and to use their loss as a stepping-stone to renewal, growth, and even transformation.

Carmel Valley, California
January 1980

PART ONE

Introduction to Grief

1
The Courage to Grieve

And ever has it been that love knows not
its own depth until the hour of separation.
                                        —The Prophet

The death of a loved one is the most profound of all sorrows.
The grief that comes with such a loss is intense and multifaceted,
affecting our emotions, our bodies, and our lives. Grief is preoccu-
pying and depleting. Emotionally, grief is a mixture of raw feelings
such as sorrow, anguish, anger, regret, longing, fear, and deprivation. Grief may be experienced physically as exhaustion, emptiness, tension, sleeplessness, or loss of appetite. Grief invades our
daily lives in many sudden gaps and changes, like that empty
place at the dinner table, or the sudden loss of affection and
companionship, as well as in many new apprehensions, adjustments, and uncertainties. The loss of a loved one throws every
aspect of our lives out of balance. The closer we were to the
person who died, the more havoc the loss creates. Love does
not die quickly. Hence to grieve is also "to celebrate the depth
of the union. Tears are then the jewels of remembrance, sad but
glistening with the beauty of the past. So grief in its bitterness
marks the end . . . but it also is praise to the one who is gone."
     During the months of mourning after a death, we learn to
face the reality and the pain of our loss, to say good-bye to
the dead loved one, to restore ourselves, and to reinvest in life
once again. In a sense, mourning is a time of new mastery over
ourselves and our lives. Recovery comes in the days ahead, when
mourning is completed and a new balance is found. But before
we recover we have many experiences that trigger our grief anew

until those feelings truly dissipate. Finishing or completing grief comes when we are able to let go of our feelings of grief and our intense connection with the deceased. Although our love never dies, the pain of our loss can eventually dissolve.

Although we may feel ignorant about grief, grief is in fact like a neighbor who always lives next door, no matter where or how we live, no matter how we try to move away. Grief may result from any significant change or loss in our lives. Whether we want to or not, every one of us has to learn to let go, to move forward without someone or something we wanted very much.

Life is change. We undergo change, loss, and grief from birth onward. Every venture from home, every move, every job or status change, every loss of a person, pet, belief, every illness, every shift in life such as marriage, divorce, or retirement, and every kind of personal growth and change may be cause for grief. These are what Elisabeth Kübler-Ross calls the "little deaths" of life.

If we would face everyday changes and practice letting go in our daily lives, perhaps loss and grief would be less traumatic. Even though we have a multitude of opportunities for learning how to handle grief, we usually avoid our feelings of loss. We bear up and force ourselves onward. Because we deny the full measure of our grief in our everyday changes and losses, when the big griefs come then grief feels unfamiliar, frightening, and overwhelming. Nonetheless, the death of a loved one is so great and so final a loss that our past experiences with "little deaths" may never adequately prepare us.

Most of us have had some experience with healthy grieving. For example, although we often feel isolated in our personal grief, mourners across our nation were helped together to work through their grief when President Kennedy was assassinated. On television we saw images of Kennedy, his life, the circumstances of his death, and his funeral over and over again for several days. We talked with each other about the loss of our president. We read about his life. This then is the essential process of grieving—repeating again and again the images of, and feelings about, our lost loved one until the mourning process is completed.

That we can grieve and recover often seems an amazing feat, yet human resilience is amazing. Just as a forest can burn to the ground and eventually grow anew, or a town can be devastated by a flood and rebuild, so each of us can be overcome by our grief, have the enormity of our loss overwhelm us, and still eventually recover and restore our lives. This is nature's way. This book is as much about recovery, completion, and restoration as it is about the grief experience itself. This is a book of hope. Even though at times it may seem impossible, we can conquer grief, heal, and even grow from the experience.

Grief is a wound that needs attention in order to heal. To work through and complete grief means to face our feelings openly and honestly, to express or release our feelings fully, and to tolerate and accept our feelings for however long it takes for the wound to heal. For most of us, that is a big order. Therefore, it takes courage to grieve. It takes courage to feel our pain and to face the unfamiliar. It also takes courage to grieve in a society that mistakenly values restraint, where we risk the rejection of others by being open or different. Open mourners are a select group, willing to journey into pain and sorrow and anger in order to heal and recover.

Unfortunately, our misconceptions about grief keep us from developing the courage we need to face grief. Many of us fear that, if allowed in, grief will bowl us over indefinitely. The truth is that grief experienced does dissolve. The only grief that does not end is grief that has not been fully faced. Grief unexpressed is like a powder keg waiting to be ignited. We also misunderstand tears. A slang expression for crying in our society is "to break down." We act as if weeping is wrong or akin to illness, while tears actually afford us a necessary release of our intense feelings. Another misconception is that if we truly loved someone, we will never finish with our grief, as if continued sorrow is a testimonial to our love. But true love does not need grief to support its truth. Love can last in a more healthy and meaningful way, once our grief is dispelled. We can honor our dead more by the quality of our continued living than by our constantly remembering the past. Another common misconception is that grief cannot be finished. The falsity of this notion will be confirmed later, in chapter 12. Finally, there is a popular belief that self-neglect is part of grief. Healthy grief, however, relies on self-care. Self-neglect is no testimonial to love. Instead, our deceased loved one would want us to love ourselves, as he or she loved us.

How do we learn to have the courage to grieve? Some of us learn courage spontaneously, when we must act in order to survive. Most of us learn the courage to face new challenges in the process of living, experiencing and surviving our struggles over and over again. Since pain is unavoidable, we can learn to make pain our teacher instead of our enemy. As George Bernard Shaw so aptly said, "Heartbreak is life educating us." We can learn that courage makes our path more challenging, exciting, and rewarding.

One way to learn courage is to experiment with being courageous. A beautiful example of this was given to me by my friend Tom, who at age forty was told by his physician that he had lung cancer. Tom was terrified. Then he thought about the woman he loved and how frightened she would be if he gave in to the panic inside himself. As an experiment, he decided to pretend to be courageous for her benefit. Soon he found that he was strong and courageous for himself as well, ready to face the surgery and the long recovery afterward.

Each of us, too, can learn to be courageous by experimenting with courage. We can taste courage, notice courage, pretend courage, and most of all we can try it out for ourselves. Having the courage to grieve leads to having the courage to live, to love, to risk, and to enjoy all the fruits of life without fear or inhibition. For many of us it is our fear of loss, and the grief implicit in loss, that prevents us from fully living our lives.

In many cases it is our lack of knowledge about grief that increases our fear, despair, hopelessness, and helplessness when we face a major loss in our lives. Hence, the purpose of this book is to increase our understanding and acceptance of grief as a normal, inevitable life experience. We can each learn to trust that although grief is painful, it is healthy and surmountable, and that grieving fully will enable us not only to recover but also to expand and grow. My wish is that from reading this book we will begin to develop the courage to grieve.

2
Grief and Death

You shall be free indeed when your days
are not without a care nor your nights
without a want and a grief,
But rather when these things girdle your life
and yet you rise above them naked and unbound.
—The Prophet

ACCEPTING DEATH AS REALITY

Death is a natural part of living, yet we act as if death is an outrage. We see death as our enemy; we see ourselves as death's potential victims. Each of us will die. It is simply a matter of time. Each of us is like an artist working with an unknown deadline, which is our death sentence. How can we learn to accept death as natural? "If you can begin to see death as an invisible, but friendly, companion on your life's journey—gently reminding you not to wait till tomorrow to do what you mean to do— than you can learn to *live* your life rather than simply passing through it."

Unfortunately, because we deny the existence of death we make it all the more frightening and difficult to face. Our own death is unimaginable. We have "a curious conviction . . . [that we are] immortal. We can't really imagine ourselves dead. When you dream about death, you dream you are a perceiving dead person, and not a person who is nonexistent." Our denial is supported by our rarely seeing natural human deaths. Many deaths take place out of our view in hospitals and nursing homes. What we do see daily are violent deaths on television, the results of murder, war, and accidents. Death is thus dramatized as unnatural, unexpected, and horrible. Elisabeth Kübler-Ross notes, "In our unconscious mind we can only be killed; it is inconceivable to die of a natural cause or of old age."

We also deny death by not talking about it. "We continue to share with our remotest ancestors the most tangled and evasive attitudes about death. . . . We have as much distaste for talking about personal death as for thinking about it. It is an indelicacy, like talking in mixed company about venereal disease or abortion in the old days."

Denial of death creates many problems for us. "It is the denial of death that is partially responsible for people living empty, purposeless lives; for when you live as if you'll live forever, it becomes too easy to postpone the things you know that you must do. You live your life in preparation for tomorrow or in remembrance of yesterday, and meanwhile, each today is lost."

If we do not deny death, we fear it. We may have a healthy respect for death or for time running out on us, or we may worry too much about danger, illness, or aging. Some of us spend inordinate amounts of time contemplating death, even terrorizing ourselves, in order to gain the upper hand over this frightening phenomenon. Invariably, we make ourselves miserable rather than more powerful. Like denial, the fear of death not only makes it hard for us to confront loss and death in our lives, but it may prevent us from fully living, from loving, and from risking.

Somewhere among the denial of death, the obsessive fear of death, and the contemplation of suicide is a healthy awareness and acceptance of death as a natural reality that gives our lives context and meaning. Viktor Frankl writes, "The meaning of human existence is based on its irreversible quality." Mastery of our fear of death enables us to admit that we will die, which then gives us an opportunity for making our lives more meaningful *now*. Expecting that we will die, we cannot as easily take life for granted or put off living until some unsure future. We are more apt to take action and live our lives fully.

Peter Koestenbaum suggests some philosophic values resulting from the acceptance of death:

1. We need death in order to savor life.
2. Death is an "invention" needed and therefore created for the sake of feeling alive.
3. Death puts us in touch with the sense of a real, individual existence.
4. Death makes possible decisions for authenticity—that is, courage and integrity.
5. Death gives us the strength to make major decisions.
6. Death reveals the importance of intimacy in life.
7. Death helps us ascribe meaning to our lives retroactively, a useful concept for older people.
8. Death shows us the importance of ego-transcending achievements.
9. Death shows us the path to self-esteem. It gives us the capacity to do something important.

FACING THE DEATH OF A LOVED ONE

Regardless of how it occurs, the death of a loved one is shocking, painful, and seemingly impossible to accept. We often feel unprepared and therefore devastated by the death. Our loss is compounded by our characteristic human difficulty in separating from one another; death is the supreme separation. Whatever the circumstances, confronting death is not easy.

Our grief may be affected by our loved one's age and stage in life. We tend to tolerate our loss better when we feel the deceased had a chance for some important kind of completion in his or her life. The death of a child, which seems the most unnatural of deaths, is often the most anguishing to face. Talking about the death of a young person, Viktor Frankl notes, "We cannot, after all, judge a biography by its length, by the number of pages in it; we must judge by the richness of the contents.

. . . Sometimes the 'unfinisheds' are among the most beautiful symphonies."

How our loved one dies will have a powerful effect on how we grieve. Sudden deaths, especially violent or accidental deaths, provoke our greatest shock, anxiety, and distress. Violent deaths make us feel vulnerable and fearful. Such deaths may provoke our rage or indignation at the injustice of the death. Suicide, too, has a tragic, shocking quality. Suicide may arouse unfounded guilt or a sense of failure among the survivors. Peaceful, sudden deaths, such as dying in one's sleep, seem more like a blessing, for we imagine this as an easy passage for the deceased. However, any sudden death provokes many questions, doubts, and concerns. We wonder why the death happened. Who is to blame? Could it have been prevented? Sudden deaths feel unnatural. We preoccupy ourselves with "if onlys," ruminations in which we try to rewrite history to erase this disaster. Because we are so unprepared for loss in a sudden death, and because we usually have so much unfinished business with the deceased, sudden deaths seem to be the hardest with which to cope.

Watching a lingering death can also be agonizing. To see a loved one in pain and to be helpless to ease the suffering is an anguishing experience. It is also hard to live with what feels like a death sentence and then a reprieve, repeated again and again, in some long illnesses. Day-in-and-day-out care of a dying loved one can be very draining and stressful. Death, then, may come as a relief.

Lingering deaths can be easier to face, however, because we have the opportunity to confront dying and death directly. In a lingering death, loved ones can give comfort, support, and companionship, which can ease the pain for the person dying. It is a profound experience for the survivor to be able to give in this way, just as it is of enormous solace for the one who is dying. To share the dying process with a loved one is to spare him or her the isolation and loneliness so characteristic of the dying process in our society. All involved have an opportunity to be close, to intensify their love, to share their feelings, and to come to some kind of resolution with one another before death occurs. Some of the grieving of the survivors can be accomplished in advance of the death if they are open and honest during this process. And an expected death gives the dying patient a chance to complete grieving over his own death.

The loved one who is dying may be ourself. We have to face our own death as well. We have the same choices as in facing any loss, whether to be conscious and expressive or to deny and avoid the truth. Most moving are Arleen Lorrance's ideas on facing our dying:

> Dying is a time which calls for your active participation in the process. Prepare yourself for the shift in consciousness that will occur; know what is taking place in you as it happens. Read the experiences of others. Seek out someone who can be with you while you make the transition represented by death, who can talk with you as you cross over, who can journey part of the way with you. Share the ecstasy and illumination of your death with a loved one, just as you shared the incredible joy of your birth with one or both of your parents. . . . At least be comforted that there are persons in the world who know death to be ecstasy. . . . Why be frightened in advance of the unknown? When it becomes known, it might not be frightening at all.

It is tragic that so many of those dying in our society have been isolated in hospitals and nursing homes, kept far from sight, so that medical personnel and families alike can avoid confronting the dying process. Elisabeth Kübler-Ross has been instrumental in helping to break through this denial of death in hospitals through her extensive work with the dying. Stemming in large measure from her provocation, the hospice movement has begun in this country, offering homelike facilities, where the dying, their families, and the staff can be companions in the dying process rather than dooming the dying to isolation and loneliness. In the hospice, death is dealt with as something expected, something planned for, rather than something to be feared and dreaded.

SPECIAL STRENGTHS THAT HELP US FACE DEATH

Knowledge, emotional maturity, our support system, our purpose in life, and our courage are all strengths that help us cope with life and with death. In many cases denial is simply naïveté, a defense against fear, but knowledge can be the antidote for these. "Information seeking is an essential part of the mentally healthy effort of adapting to a crisis situation." Educating ourselves about death may prevent us from feeling overwhelmed or devastated when we must face the death of a loved one.

Emotional maturity is another strength we can use in preparing to confront death. Emotional maturity is the willingness to acknowledge and cope with reality, to experience and express our feelings; it is also a kind of resilience, a capacity to bounce back to "normal" after we have faced stress. Life continually makes new and different demands on us, and all these demands are really opportunities for us to develop emotional maturity. Unfortunately, because we often try to avoid the new or the difficult or the challenging, we do not always take advantage of the opportunities to develop our abilities to cope. However, the option to mature is open to us at any time in our lives. Even children can handle death with maturity if they are dealt with honestly and supported in their grieving.

Having a life purpose, ascribing meaning to our lives, is a way of strengthening our everyday existence and giving us support in moments of crisis. This was dramatically shown by Viktor Frankl, the eminent psychiatrist who survived the horrors of years in a Nazi concentration camp by focusing on his life as purposeful, on his dignity as a human being, on his love, and on what he intended to accomplish in the future.

Our support system is another strength that enables us to face loss and death more readily. This includes the network of people and activities that fill our lives, as well as the understanding and support we give to ourselves. This aspect of our lives is examined in depth in chapter 10.

Finally, courage is one of the greatest assets we can possess for facing life and death. Even the most uncourageous of us can learn courage. Anytime we are willing to take a risk is a step toward courage. Whenever we face anything difficult without running away, we are courageous. Having the courage to face sorrow, disappointment, and hardship invariably generates a much more rewarding life. Having the courage to confront death with honesty inevitably means that we examine our lives, our values, our ideas, and our sense of meaning, so that eventually we can create an existence that has satisfaction and purpose. By accepting death as a natural life process, we can live our lives with more zest and depth, and we can achieve the greatest richness possible. In other words, the courage to accept death will enhance our lives.

In order to develop the courage to face death squarely, most of us will need help to break through our own denial of death. Chapter 15 is devoted to discussion and exercises designed to penetrate our denial and to help us begin to accept death as a natural phenomenon in our lives.

PART TWO

The Grief Experience

3
The Mourning Period

And you would accept the seasons of your heart,
even as you have always accepted the seasons
that pass over your fields.
And you would watch with serenity
through the winters of your grief.
                              —The Prophet

Whenever we lose a loved one, we grieve: for weeks, for several months, or even for a period of years. This time for grieving is called the mourning period, first described by Sigmund Freud in his 1917 paper "Mourning and Melancholia." Although there is no set time, many cultures and religions designate one year for mourning. There is a wisdom in the traditional one year of mourning, which enables the bereaved to take at least some of the time necessary to experience and complete the grieving process. In one year we can begin to learn to live with the absence of our loved one at each of the difficult special occasions like birthdays, anniversaries, and Christmas. Since grief is so painful and hard to sustain, we tend to push ourselves to finish grieving long before we are ready. A full year allows us to move toward and away from our grief over and over again, as we aim toward completion. However, a year may not be nearly enough time, and we each will heal in our own unique time frame.

The mourning period is really a time of convalescence. It is a time for facing the loss and all the feelings that the loss evokes in order at least to begin to heal the great wound created by the death of a loved one. This is a time when every aspect of our relationship with the deceased—our attachment, feelings, thoughts, and memories, as well as our past, present, and future—is examined and re-examined over and over again. The purpose of this mourning period is for us to heal, to recover, and to regain our equilibrium and our capacity for living fully once again.

Even in those rare instances when we feel prepared in advance for the death of a loved one, we are seldom prepared for the changes a loss makes in our everyday lives. Coping with these changes is another important task of the mourning period. Where our life was connected to another's, there is a huge gap when the other is gone. This great loss creates smaller painful everyday losses. One widow told me, "Before my husband died, everything was clearly set out for me. Suddenly at sixty-nine I have nothing to do, no sense of purpose." Abruptly having to begin redefining our lives and creating new meaning and purpose can seem an enormous task.

Wounds do not heal without time and attention. Yet too many of us feel that we don't have the right to take time to heal from emotional or psychical wounds. Ideally we should not push ourselves too quickly back into our regular routine lest we accentuate our pain. However, most of us do not have the luxury of withdrawing from our responsibilities, so it is essential that we not expect too much of ourselves. Since loss makes life feel quite abnormal, trying to resume "normal" routine too quickly after a death can be a very difficult endeavor.

There are two major psychological tasks to be accomplished during the mourning period. The first is to acknowledge and accept the truth: that death has occurred and that the relationship is now over. The second task is to experience and deal with all the emotions and problems this loss creates for the bereaved. These tasks intertwine. Each takes time. Each is necessary for the eventual recovery from grief.

While we are mourning, our grief is in the foreground and most other aspects of life move to the background. One woman described her experience of mourning this way: "At first I felt as if my loss was like a spotlight in front of my eyes all the time. I couldn't see anything but the spotlight. I was blinded by it. As time passed, the light moved farther from my eyes, and I could see what was around it and behind it. Now, months later, the spotlight is out of sight much of the time. I know it still exists, but I am no longer conscious of it all the time."

Mourning is one time in life when we are apt to feel we have a right to put everything else aside. For many of us, suspension from activities and freedom from functioning are essential and a source of great relief. We may need to do nothing for weeks, perhaps for the first time in our lives. For others of us the gaps in time and activity may accentuate our loss too painfully. We then cannot tolerate nothingness and need to continue functioning throughout our grief. It is important to realize that we are not all alike in how we grieve. Just as each of us must grieve in our own individual way, so our needs and reactions may not be the same each time we confront a loss.

Feelings of grief are very intense and often very mixed. We may feel emotions in an entirely new or different way. Among the many feelings aroused by loss are sorrow, anguish, disbelief, despair, anxiety, loneliness, guilt, regret, resentment, emptiness, and numbness, as well as yearning, love, and appreciation for the deceased. All these are natural feelings of grief that may occur together or at different times. For the sake of maintaining our emotional health, it is important for us to admit our feelings, not deny them. We must learn to tolerate and accept our emotions as well as the loss itself. Erich Lindemann suggests that each feeling in grief must be "pained through." This, to be sure, is not an easy task.

Emotional pain is not constant, even though we sometimes think it is. Emotional pain feels constant only when all our energy is going into suppressing those feelings that are so hard to suppress. We cannot tolerate the continual onslaught of emotional pain. The natural process in grieving involves experiencing times of intense feeling and then following them with periods of quiet. Allowing ourselves to move naturally in and out of pain, instead of forcing artificial controls on our feelings, enables us to go through and complete the grief process more quickly. In other words, confronting grief rather than avoiding it shortens the duration of the experience. Some of us let our feelings out fully and openly because we instinctively know that this is right for us. But without understanding why we are doing so, others of us feel *compelled* to express ourselves in this way. For some this degree of openness will be a new experience, perhaps an awkward one, and even an extremely difficult undertaking.

In order to mourn completely, we must realize our needs. We need, first of all, to take the time to grieve. We need to talk and to cry as much as we can. We need an environment, or people around us, that supports our grieving rather than inhibits us. We need to be free from major decisions if we feel unsure or unready for them. What is hardest about mourning for many of us is that this is a time when we naturally need so much. It is important that we honor our needs and know that we are being not self-indulgent but instead self-supporting.

In the next three chapters we will talk about each phase of grief. But we must remember that while the three phases are separated for the purpose of discussion here, grief itself does not move with such precision. Each of us will experience the phases of grief in our own way.

4

The First Phase of Grief: Shock

And of nights when earth was upwrought
with confusion.
                    —The Prophet

Before we recover from grief we go through many different moods
and reactions in order to come to terms with death and loss.
There are several phases of grief between the initial disbelief
and the ultimate acceptance of the death. Hope for reunion is
given up slowly. Memories, ideas, and feelings are collected and
relinquished again and again until mourning is completed.

For most of us there are three major stages in the mourning
process. The first phase is one of shock or numbness that may
last for hours, days, or even weeks. The second and longest phase,
which may last for months, is a period of suffering and disorganization. The last phase is a period of reorganization.

"I can't believe it!" is often our first reaction to hearing of a
death. The death of a loved one is always unbelievable. We do
not want the death to be true. It is much the same as living
out a nightmare, for the fact of death feels unreal and impossible.

When we are shocked, we go numb to some extent. Then we
become suspended in a state of unreality, only vaguely aware
of what is going on around us. Some of our pain is shut off, as
if we are partially anesthetized. Experiences are blurred or hazy.
We seem to be living as if in a dream. Our whole organism creates
this natural protection against facing all at once the full impact
of our loss. Just as the body goes into shock after an accident
or injury, so the mind goes into shock when faced with severe
emotional crises. This numbness or anesthesia is temporary. The

length of time is unpredictable, but shock may last for days or weeks. The numbness initially insulates us from the intensity of our feelings, but it may also prevent us from grasping right away the full significance of the loss.

Sometimes panic alternates with numbness. We may suddenly feel frightened that we cannot remember what our dead loved one looked like, or afraid that we cannot go on alone now. It is important that these sudden jolts be tempered, to ease us slowly into facing the reality of our loss. Hence, numbness is a necessary aspect of the early days of grieving.

Our numbness sometimes enables us to cope with the myriad of details that need to be faced immediately after the death of a loved one. These activities and the people who share our lives often keep us going during the first days of mourning.

Although the bereaved often remember little of the period of shock after a death, many remember their anger, which is sometimes irrational and uncontrolled. Though sorrow and pain are masked for us in shock, anger may lash out freely, unexpectedly, at almost any target. Anger is one of few outlets we have for the disbelief, frustration, and helplessness we feel when we are confronted by a death. Anger also provokes moments of aliveness in what is ordinarily a time of numbness. Despite the fact that under these circumstances anger may feel uncomfortable and startling, we need to accept it as natural.

People in shock sometimes look stoical, as if they are coping without much emotion. The truth is that in shock we do not feel the full impact of loss and that therefore we are not yet suffering as we will once the numbness wears off. Observing someone who is in great pain acting in a stoical, seemingly unemotional way can be a bewildering experience. But this apparent stoicism is actually a robotlike way of functioning. To be able to function at all may reassure us that we are coping and not falling apart at the impact of our loss. For example, a friend's mother chattered incessantly about inconsequential matters for days after her husband died. Finally, in utter frustration, my friend asked his mother to spend some quiet time alone with him. His mother said indignantly, "I can't be quiet or I'll cry."

For Diane Kennedy Pike, wife of Bishop James Pike, it was during the period of shock that she recorded all the events that preceded her husband's death in the Israeli wilderness. She actually created her book *Search* during the first weeks of her grief, before she fully acknowledged her suffering.

Even after we recover from the initial shock of loss, there will be times in the coming days and months when we again feel "I can't believe it!" Our psyches scrutinize the actuality of death over and over, attempting to accept and integrate the loss into our lives. Because death is usually a fact we do not want to believe, it is a long, slow process to overcome our resistance and accept reality. The truth is that we keep hoping we will awaken from this nightmare.

5

The Middle Phase of Grief: Suffering and Disorganization

When you are sorrowful look again in
your heart, and you shall see that in truth
you are weeping for that which has been
your delight.

—The Prophet

When the shock wears off, as if emerging from a trance, we begin to experience the full impact and pain of facing the finality of our loss. This is a time of the greatest suffering. Diane Kennedy Pike described the loss of a loved one as like having a tree that had been growing in one's heart suddenly yanked out by its roots, leaving a gaping hole or wound. The pain is intense but not constant. Both the emotions that accompany a loss—unbalancing, overwhelming, and as new and as different as they may be—and the actual life changes caused by the death are disorganizing for us.

It is natural now for us to weep a great deal. Tears are nature's way of helping us express and release our pain. We may ruminate over and be intensely preoccupied with the details of the lost loved one's life or death, over our relationship with one another, over our memories, over our last encounter, over unfinished business together, or even over our more abstract ideas about death. So bewildered are we by the fact of death that many of us become preoccupied for a time with deep questions about *why* the loved one died. And because grief exaggerates the positive and negative aspects of our relationship, we are apt to go over and over those aspects in our minds. "Hostile relationships and quarrels which have not been redeemed are just as difficult an aspect of grieving as loving relationships."

Our minds may seem to work intensely fast, covering all the details that relate to the deceased. One man told me after his son had died that at first he seemed to think of his son "eight hundred times a day," no matter what he was doing to keep himself busy. Ruminating is simply part of the healing process.

Yet as busy as our minds may be in one sense, in another sense we may feel blank, out in space, unable to focus or concentrate. Sometimes we will hear and respond to other people. At other times we may feel unable to respond at all, which accentuates our sense of isolation from those around us.

Emotionally we feel acute suffering, even hysteria at times. Such intensity of feeling may be new to us. We may find such emotions as bitterness, anger, self-pity, and guilt especially hard to acknowledge. Although we may be bewildered or disturbed by our emotions, we need to realize that this is the way in which grief affects most people. We may feel unprepared to cope with so much emotion, or we may feel inadequate to the task. Our doubts about our capacity to cope may cause a temporary diminishing of our self-esteem, just as certain uncomfortable feelings such as guilt or resentment can cause us momentarily to feel badly about ourselves during the grieving process.

Likewise, a sense of impoverishment is characteristic of mourning. Therefore, at this painful time companionship is our greatest need. We may need others to listen to us, to talk to us, to hold us, even to take over for us. This new onslaught of needs can be very uncomfortable, even frightening, yet it confirms how different mourning is from normal times. Facing a death is such an emotional crisis that it is natural for us to feel needy, depleted, and overwhelmed as well as unable to cope or function for a while. If this needy time occurs when we are alone and without support, our needs may seem even more greatly intensified.

Depression and grief are inextricably linked. We are naturally depressed when grieving. Depressed, we feel irritable, dejected in spirits, withdrawn, unresponsive, apathetic, unable to concentrate, powerless, and lacking in confidence. Loss of appetite and extreme fatigue are also symptomatic of depression and grief. So much of our energy is tied up inside that little energy is available for action or functioning. We may be moody. At times we may feel pain and weep, and then at other times we may feel detached and without emotion. During this period we may be withdrawn and unable to relate to other people. Negativity, pessimism, emptiness, and a temporary sense of the meaninglessness of life are all symptoms of depression. "What's the use?" or "Why bother?" are typical feelings. We may be acutely restless and then become immobile. Feelings vary, of course, and not everyone will feel all the emotions mentioned. The essential thing to remember is that the pain of grief is never constant and does not last forever. Throughout this middle phase of mourning, the myriad of feelings of grief come and go in waves, with lessening intensity as time goes on.

Thoughts of suicide are not unusual when a person is grieving. It is important to understand, however, that these are just thoughts, that we are not going to act on them. The wish to die is partly a wish for reunion with the dead loved one. Thoughts of dying are also an imaginary way to gain relief from the pain of grief. Suicidal thoughts may be the result of unexpressed guilt or anger, and they serve as self-punishing ideas. Since life does not seem very meaningful at the time of mourning, it is natural to consider death as an alternative. Considering suicide is also one way to come to terms with the fact of loss and death. The thinking is something like this: If I can consider and tolerate the idea of my own death, perhaps death itself will not seem so frightening or so hard for me to endure. Maybe then I'll accept this loss. As we come to accept the loss of the loved one, the suicidal thoughts disappear.

Our sleep is usually affected whenever we face severe emotional crises of any kind. Almost every person who is in the midst of intense grief has some difficulty sleeping. Problems with sleep result from the great strain of the psychological work involved in grief. In normal times we work out many of our psychic problems during sleep. Grief creates an overload, more work than the psyche can comfortably handle either in sleep or in waking time. Insomnia is common. There are several types of insomnia. Difficulty falling asleep is one form. Frequently, obsessive thinking can keep us awake. Because we often equate falling asleep with dying, while we are grieving we may be fearful of falling asleep. Another kind of insomnia is waking up frequently, or awakening fully after only a few hours of sleep, unable to sleep more. It is also common while mourning to sleep long hours and yet never feel fully rested.

Dreaming may also be affected during the mourning period. Dreams are a major means of re-experiencing and working through emotionally charged experiences and of problem-solving. Much grief work gets done in our sleep. Unpleasant dreams or nightmares may occur at any time in our lives, but they may be more memorable or more disturbing when we are grieving and vulnerable. In contrast, not remembering dreams, even feeling anesthetized through the night, is not unusual during mourning. After a loved one dies, it is quite natural to dream about that person, often as if they never died at all. Dreams sometimes express our wishes. Dreaming about the loved one is another way to begin to accept the death, distressing as it is to awaken again to the reality of death. One client of mine said, "As painful as it is to dream about my dead child, it is wonderful to be able to be with him again, at least in my sleep." It was certainly reassuring to me to maintain some kind of contact with my brother through dreams, long after his death.

During the mourning period it is important to rest, in order to renew our energy, keep up our strength, and maintain our health, even if we are unable to sleep a lot. We are much more vulnerable to illness and infection when our energy is depleted, as it is during the grieving process. Sometimes while grieving we mistakenly believe we should let ourselves go physically, when in fact the opposite is true.

We may lose interest in food and eating. The most extreme form of this is called anorexia, which is the inability to eat at all. Weight loss is common during bereavement. However, we may eat more under the stress of grief, and sometimes chronic hunger persists even after eating. We need to be sure we have a healthy diet that includes plenty of protein. When distressed, we often eat poorly, turning to carbohydrates and sugars, which, as immediately satisfying foods, are not as sustaining as proteins. Vitamin C and a stress vitamin regimen may also help. For further assistance in this regard we might consult someone knowledgeable about nutrition and health.

When depressed or anxious we sometimes develop physical symptoms such as dizziness, trembling, shortness of breath, headaches, heartburn, and new aches and pains, as well as the fatigue that typifies grief. Some mourners seem to have a chronic cold. These are stress reactions similar to the sleep difficulties characteristic of the mourning period.

We may also become obsessively preoccupied with our health and body functions after a loved one dies, which is also a natural outgrowth of grief. Facing a death can bring to awareness all our fears of death. Some of us may temporarily develop symptoms that imitate the illness of the deceased.

Sexuality is also deeply affected by grief. After the loss of a spouse, sexual frustration may be an intense source of anguish. But there is also a natural emotional withdrawal during mourning that may cause a diminishing or a total loss of interest in sex. Sometimes the pleasure of intimacy may produce guilt or anxiety during the initial weeks of mourning, or we may find our sexual needs intensified along with our other needs. Confusion reigns when we are torn between the need and wish for closeness on one hand, and detachment and lack of sexual responsiveness on the other. Masturbation may help diminish sexual tension and frustration. Sexual dysfunctions of various kinds, such as impotence and premature ejaculation in men, and inability to respond or attain orgasm in women, occur during the early months of bereavement. Symptoms in the sensitive area of sexuality usually subside with understanding, tolerance, and patience. Everyone who grieves eventually recovers sexuality, but the recovery time is variable.

Loneliness and yearning are common in bereavement. Death leaves a hole in life that we feel very deeply. At first it is natural to think that no one—nothing—can ever fill that void. Each person we love is unique to us. The loss is all the more keenly felt because of the specialness of the loved one and our relationship with each other. The death also may have left us with new responsibilities which were formerly handled by the deceased. Each of these new jobs may intensify our loneliness and sense of loss. We will frequently wish the death was a lie, a mistake. We may yearn for the deceased to return to us and for life to return to "normal." Loneliness, painful as it is, indicates that we are allowing ourselves to acknowledge the truth. In coming to terms with a death, we periodically suffer from loneliness, yearning, and feeling the painful gap in our lives. As we heal, these feelings lessen and eventually disappear.

The feeling of abandonment is one of the most agonizing feelings we must endure and conquer in grief. Whatever the circumstances, we tend to experience a loved one's death as an abandonment. Our imaginations toy with the idea that "if he had loved me, he would not have died." Temporarily we feel deserted, unwanted, and unloved. Sometimes we feel plagued with feelings of worthlessness that seem to justify our loved one's leaving us.

Guilt and the consequent self-reproach are invariably feelings that we must confront. We are so susceptible to guilt after a loss that we can turn any thought, feeling, experience, or memory to guilt. Some of us are obsessed with guilt, and others feel guilt mildly. Guilt may serve to deny the reality of the death. Being a "survivor" provokes guilt. We wonder, "Why am I alive and not him?" Then we feel blessed, frightened, relieved, and regretful all at once. These mixed feelings within the depths of sorrow confuse us and cause self-reproach.

When we have actually survived in a situation where others died, such as in an accident or wartime, we are apt to suffer deep trauma. In addition to intense survivor guilt, we may be plagued by rage, depression, and fear for many months. Psychotherapy may be essential to help the survivor recover.

Another painful kind of guilt may come when the death has brought us some kind of relief. This can occur especially when the relationship with the loved one was somehow difficult, or when the deceased was ill for a long time before the death. We may have wished for respite from the dying process, and when death occurs we are naturally relieved.

Frequently, too, we feel guilt about the last moments, days, or weeks of the relationship. We may immediately regret some word spoken or something unsaid or undone. We may remember minute details of the last encounter and torment ourselves with worry about them. Or we may regret something we did or something we failed to do. For example, several people have shared with me their guilt at being unable to be honest with the person dying and tell him that this was actually the end. Some failure in the relationship may cause us to berate ourselves.

Many kinds of unfinished business with the deceased appear later on in the form of guilt. During mourning, "shoulds" and "if onlys" rise to the surface. Some of us torment ourselves endlessly with these issues. Yet any thought we have can be turned into an "if only" statement. Here are some kinds of "if onlys" that can follow the death of a loved one, depending on the relationship and circumstances of the death:

If only I had known she was dying . . .
If only I had made him quit smoking . . .
If only I had forbidden her to drive . . .
If only he hadn't taken that trip . . .
If only I had gone with her . . .

If only he had seen his physician more regularly . . .
If only I had insisted she work shorter hours . . .
If only I had taken his symptoms more seriously . . .

Then there are the "if onlys" about changing reality:
If only I hadn't fought with him so much about money . . .
If only I had been more loving . . .
If only we hadn't moved . . .
If only he hadn't retired . . .
If only we had had more children . . .
If only I had been stricter . . .
If only I hadn't nagged him . . .

Anything at all can become an "if only." Our unfulfilled wishes as well as our mistakes can cause us great pain. But when we imagine that if we had acted differently we might have prevented the death, we figuratively endow ourselves with superhuman powers to change destiny. How unrealistic we are to burden ourselves with unnatural responsibility for the death. Yet we all do this to some extent. Each of us is convinced for a time that changing our behavior might have altered reality. Everyone facing a loss has some "if onlys." However, our guilt is an exercise in futility. We cannot go backward. Instead we must let go and forgive ourselves.

When the "if onlys" become obsessive and persist for years, the survivor is suffering a pathological problem. Some survivors are so plagued with the death that they keep imagining and re-arranging the whole history of the deceased, as if the survivor could stack the cards in a direction other than death. Obsessively recreating the life and death of the deceased is a way to deny the reality.

Guilt feelings often arise when we were not present when death occurred. We may feel cheated out of our last moments with the loved one. It is a profound sorrow to imagine that we have let the loved one down in some major way, that perhaps our presence might have eased their death. There may be a fantasy of omnipotence inherent in this guilt: "If I had been there, he/she might not have died." This belief counters the deep sense of impotence we feel when a loved one dies.

Unresolved guilt is common in grief. Dealing with the guilt is essential, for guilt can undermine self-confidence and delay one's recovery. Guilt can even be paralyzing. We must allow ourselves to express aloud the variations of guilt and also the stories that support our guilt in order to let it go. We need to aim for a more realistic view of both the relationship with the deceased and with the death. Guilt is the emotional area in which we most commonly become trapped during the grieving process. It may persist because of our unwillingness to share the problem with anyone else. It is legitimate and often necessary for us to seek professional assistance with these feelings. The worst thing we can do is avoid confronting guilt feelings, since many physical and emotional problems may arise from stifling these emotions.

Anger, and an accompanying impulse to place blame on others, is also a common feeling during the grieving process. We may be angry at the world because we have had to suffer this loss. "Why me?" we ask. We may resent anyone who seems happy or anyone who has never had to face such a serious loss. This new anger may be frightening, and we may feel guilty about feeling angry.

Anger may recur again and again during the time we are grieving. Anger is a natural outgrowth of our sense of impotence and helplessness, our sense of disappointment and loss, and our sense of abandonment by the loved one. Granger E. Westburg, in his book *Good Grief,* aptly states the issues that arise in anger.

> When we have something precious taken from us, we inevitably go through a stage when we are very critical of everything and everyone who was related to the loss. We spare no one in our systematic scrutiny of the event, attempting to understand why this thing happened, and who is to blame. The human is always looking for someone to blame . . . we are hostile to the doctor because he operated; or we are hostile to him because he did not

operate. No matter what he did, it was wrong. While we are in this mood, we look at everyone with a jaundiced eye.

Sometimes we are unable, or unwilling, to experience anger openly and directly. Psychologists think that in many cases depression is anger that has been turned inward onto oneself instead of turned outward to the real source in the world. Many of us are more comfortable becoming depressed than being angry. Sometimes we experience frozen anger or rage. Unable to face the anger or express it, we control it and hold it inside to such an extent that we feel blocked and frozen. Indications of frozen anger or rage may be acting wooden and unemotional and feeling tight, immobile, and unmoved, persisting into a state of detachment. A simple way of checking to see if we are denying our anger is to say aloud a few times "I am angry" and see what happens. The best way to cope with feelings is to express them aloud rather than suppress them. Expressing feelings aloud gets them into the open where they can be dealt with and resolved rather than being allowed to smolder inside us and poison us.

Some of us restrain all our sorrow as well as our anger and appear frozen or wooden, creating a psychological paralysis for ourselves. Mourners who restrain their emotions too tightly may seem paralyzed. We may be unable to cry because we fear self-pity or "breaking down" and being unable to function.

Generalized fearfulness is also a common feeling after the death of someone close. We may fear being alone. Many newly bereaved find being home alone intolerable at first. Fear of loss is natural. Suddenly the world around us becomes fragile, and everyone we love seems to be in danger of dying at any minute. Feeling deserted, we fear desertion. Fearing illness or injury to ourselves or other loved ones is common, as is fearing that we or someone we love will suddenly die without warning. All these fears are an outgrowth of the shock of facing a death. The world temporarily seems less safe and more dangerous while we move to accustom ourselves to the loss. These fears tend to pass as we come to accept the loss more and more. Fears that persist months beyond the time of a loss may indicate deeper problems. Counseling or psychotherapy can help in this case.

Ambivalence is another feeling that may arise when a loved one dies. Only rarely do we feel one kind of emotion when we love. Typically, in relationships we withhold the full expression of what we appreciate and what we resent about another. When a death occurs, all our feelings—both positive and negative—are likely to intensify and rise rapidly to the surface. This experience can be both bewildering and overwhelming. For example, one new widow described the many resentments that surfaced along with her sorrow at losing the great love of her life. Positive and negative feelings are part of all our relationships. Most of us can accept such ambivalent feelings as fairly natural, except when death occurs. Then we expect all our negative feelings to vanish. But the only way to get feelings to go away is to deal with them head-on—to confront them, consider them, accept them, and then let them go.

During mourning we often try to deny our ambivalent feelings and *idealize* the loved one instead. At first we are aware only of how great our loss is. We remember just the good things and deny that we had any negative feelings about the deceased. However, extensive idealization is a way of denying feelings like anger, ambivalence, and guilt. Carried on too long, this denial makes coping with the loss and recovering all the harder to do. Instead we need to allow ourselves to remember everything about our dead loved one, even though selective memory is very tempting.

Preoccupation with the past or with the future is natural in the process of mourning. The present, fraught as it is with pain and sorrow, feels like something to be avoided. The past is when we still had our loved one, and it holds cherished memories. The future, unknown as it is, is open to our daydreams and wishes as well as to our fears and doubts. Often we involve ourselves with the future, mistakenly believing we can control it by anticipation.

Another difficult aspect of the mourning process is our habitual behavior. When we are grieving we are not likely to accept change easily. Hence, we often continue habits that preceded the death. One widow told me how she had continued to set the table for two, even though she was now alone. Embarrassed at first, she then decided to do it consciously for a few weeks, until eating alone was not so hard for her. Other examples of continuing the habits of a relationship are buying the deceased's favorite food, making an appointment for the deceased, or automatically including the deceased in some social engagement. It is as if we temporarily forget the death. Several mothers have described continuing to clean their dead child's room as usual, unable to dismantle or remove anything that was part of the habit of their living together. Breaking the habits that intertwined our lives with the deceased, like other aspects of recovering from grief, is a difficult process that takes time.

It also is hard to detach ourselves from the symbols of the loved one who is gone. Reminders seem to exist everywhere and to appear when we least expect them. Symbols are hard to deal with because they invariably reopen the wound of grief, if only for a moment. For example, listening to my brother's favorite song, "Tenderly," was both appealing and excruciatingly painful after he died. Seeing a dead child's baseball cap or prom dress, seeing a dead spouse's favorite flower or favorite book, can provoke grief anew. A friend told me after her marriage of many years had ended that she sensed she could make the whole of New York City symbolic of her lost relationship. But instead, she decided to let go of all the symbols, acting as if nothing was symbolic, which saved her considerable agony. This seems a remarkable feat that few of us can accomplish, but consciously letting go, little by little, of our attachment to the symbols of our loved one helps in our recovery from grief.

Frequently during this mourning period we may feel irrational, mentally ill, or off-balance. We may say or do or imagine out-of-the ordinary things and think we are going "crazy." This is not mental illness but a natural part of grief. We are often quite off-balance in the months following the death of a loved one. Life is askew, and our feelings and behavior may seem strange to us. We may experience new emotions, intense mixtures of feelings that burst out unexpectedly. We may feel hysterical at times, even months after our loss. Racing thoughts, confusion, inability to "think straight" or to concentrate, fear, and irrational thoughts about suicide, death, or reunion with the deceased all add to the pain and despair of mourning. Again, these are typical and temporary moments in the grieving process.

One dramatic example of this disorganized aspect of mourning was a woman named Margaret who got drunk several months after her husband had died. Margaret called a close friend on the phone and expressed worry that her husband had not yet come home from work, that he was very late. Shocked that, with alcohol, Margaret could so completely deny her husband's death, the friend went to Margaret and told her again that her husband was dead.

Similarly, months after my brother died, I was at a large family gathering when someone greeted one of the relatives at the door with "David!"—said with a great deal of feeling. I simply assumed my brother had come back to join us (from the dead) and was shocked to remember that I also had a cousin named David.

Often we imagine seeing the dead loved one on the street, and we take off after that stranger as if our loved one has returned. That we seem able to forget totally that a person is dead is certainly disturbing. For the moment this can make us feel "crazy." What is happening, however, is similar to what happens in our dreams that deny the death. Our minds are trying to cope with the trauma of the loss. For the moment, our wish or our denial is stronger than our acceptance of the reality. This temporary blindness to the truth is a natural part of grieving.

In a similar vein, during the off-balance time of mourning we sometimes do self-destructive things without really being aware of what we are doing. Injuries and accidents—such as falls or car crashes—during the mourning period typify this kind of self-destructiveness. One woman I know broke her right hand in an accident, just after her husband's death. And an unmarried woman named Carol became pregnant one month after her sister's death, adding another serious crisis to her life. In therapy, Carol and I discovered her secret motivation, which was an unconscious wish to replace her sister for herself and her family. The antidote to self-destructive behavior is to pay attention to taking good care of ourselves while grieving.

Sometimes we have feelings or experiences that seem unreal. We may hear unusual sounds, like footsteps of the absent dead person. While grieving, we may have actual visions of the deceased reappearing. Some writers call these experiences "hallucinations." That word is intimidating, implying something pathological, when in fact visions of the dead, like dreams, are fairly typical. These may seem like mystical experiences. Diane Pike described a powerful vision of her husband that indicated to her that he was not just lost in the wilderness but dead. Another woman reported that for several weeks after his death her father seemed to appear at the end of her bed laughing at her, which frightened her. One day, in asking herself what his message might be, she suddenly "heard" him say as he might have when alive, "Laugh a little. Don't take this grief so seriously." Then her visions of her father disappeared. Sometimes people "hear" a message from the deceased or feel they get some special words in a dream. In the movie *Autumn Sonata,* Liv Ullmann describes *sensing* the presence of her dead little boy. Another woman told me she felt her dead son's hand brush her face shortly after his death.

Decision-making during the mourning period is an important issue. It is ironic that while the bereaved person usually has difficulty making decisions, almost from the moment death occurs new and unusual decisions must be made regarding the funeral or the remains or life details of the person now dead. Often we have neither the energy nor the necessary know-how to decide anything. It can be even harder when the deceased was the major decision-maker and we must now assume the role. Since some decisions must be made, whether we are ready and able or not, we may need to call upon a friend or relative whose judgment we trust. Decisions that can be delayed should be put off.

The problem of decision-making is compounded by the fact that when we are depressed or apathetic we do not care what happens. Therefore, decisions that we make under the stress of loss may be different from those we would make on better days.

Loss causes enough regrets without our making choices that may add more regrets to our lives. This is particularly true of big decisions, such as moving or selling major belongings. The impulse under the stress of grieving is to get rid of the place or things that remind us of the lost loved one. Typically, we may dislike our home during mourning because of the absence of the loved one. However, in time it may be pleasurable to live in a place where we have memories we cherish. Later we may also wish to have the belongings of the loved one that earlier were too painful to behold. Many people come to regret that they gave away certain things early in their grief. Therefore, it is important that we delay such decisions whenever possible. Put items aside, out of view, to be dealt with after recovery from grief.

Often, though, certain major decisions cannot be delayed. This happened to Anne, a young widow, who was left with little money and two small children when her husband unexpectedly died. She felt panicky. She no longer could afford the high rent she was paying, yet she did not want to move. With no source of income, she had to find a job. Because the thought of moving was almost as traumatic as the loss of her spouse, I encouraged Anne not to move, to wait and to borrow for a couple of months until she saw her way ahead more clearly. So Anne borrowed money for rent and food. It took her three months to get a job and a housemate to share expenses. But now she is glad she waited and preserved her home for herself and her children.

Sometimes friends or relatives encourage the bereaved to make decisions too soon. When a friend of mine lost her daughter, several people urged her to move from the family home to avoid the agony of memories of her daughter in the house. I was aghast at this advice, for it seemed to me that such a move would create a second major loss for my friend.

But friends and relatives can be of help in taking over decision-making for the bereaved in essential ways: for example, by encouraging the person grieving to delay going back to work or to school, to take a needed vacation, or to put off disposing of the deceased's belongings. Also, the supportive encouragement to go on with life can be an essential element in recovery from grief.

The image we have of ourselves during grief tends to fall between two extremes. We may feel like someone "special," but it is more likely that we will respond to the wound of grief with the feeling that we are the victim of tragedy or loss, of abandonment, or even of destiny. Because we feel like a victim, we may feel incapacitated by the intensity of our pain and sorrow. The world confirms our sense of ourselves as victims in a variety of ways. We feel pitied. People move toward us and also away from us in new and different ways. We get ignored. We get noticed. We receive too much attention, are asked too many questions, are singled out often, sometimes too often for comfort.

Conversely, we also feel "special" while grieving. The world seems to stop for us. People wait on us or try to fill many of our everyday needs that no one even seemed to notice before. Demands on us lessen or cease. We get phone calls, visits, gifts, letters. Sometimes new people reach out to us. We feel important and cared about. This special treatment is enormously supportive. It may be the only thing that bolsters us as we face the pain of our grief.

When the world resumes and we are no longer treated as "special," there is nearly always a significant, though temporary, emotional shift. People seem to pull back from the bereaved suddenly and arbitrarily, as if the time for grieving were over and we were expected to resume our usual lives. A man whose wife had been dead five months described this experience. "Few people call me now. I'm very lonely. No one worries about my meals or how I'm managing my time. People suddenly disappeared, assuming I was fully recovered from my loss. I'm not recovered. My loneliness now seems even worse. I'm embarrassed that I miss feeling *special*." Thus, it is important in assisting the bereaved not to pull away our support too suddenly or without warning.

Occasionally some of us become so attached to this special treatment that we hold on to our grief in order to continue getting attention or in order to delay resuming our lives. Unfortunately, tragedy is one of the main paths to being noticed and cared for in our society. It takes courage to risk finding other positive ways to connect with others, just as it takes courage to resume life independently.

Mourning today is further complicated for the bereaved because they are more isolated and there are fewer mourning rituals and customs than in earlier times. People without a sustaining belief system or without strong religious convictions and connections often feel lost and lonely. One friend told of her father's anguish that he did not even know how to say a prayer for his dead wife. Another man, who once wanted to be a rabbi, found so little solace in religion after his son's death that he became vehemently antireligious. Many turn to religion successfully for solace. Death is a mystery that provokes spiritual questions. We wonder if there is a God, and what truly happens after death. We also wonder "Why me?" or "Why did he die?" Looking for deeper answers to these unknowns is part of the quest of most grieving people.

6

The Final Phase of Grief: Aftershocks and Reorganization

Ay, you are like an ocean,
And though heavy-grounded ships await
the tide upon your shores, yet, even like an
ocean, you cannot hasten your tides.
—The Prophet

After several months, when the reality of death has sunk in more deeply, our needs and the tempo of our lives begin to change. We are entering a new phase of grieving, the reorganization period. We tend to react in a different manner during this next stage. We may need more quiet and fewer people around, when up to now we have been unwilling to be alone. If we have been very quiet and withdrawn, we may now be ready to resume a more active social life. It may now be harder to just sit around. We may feel more urgency to fill the gap the loss has made in our lives. We may need more fulfilling activity, more involvement in life. However, our need to express ourselves continues throughout the entire mourning process, whether we honor that need or not.

We can see we are moving closer to recovery from grief when the deceased is no longer our primary focus. With time, this change occurs naturally, but it can be distressing rather than welcome if we mistakenly believe that our love for the deceased is measured by the strength of our sorrow. It is important to clear ourselves of misconceptions like this one so that we can fully reorganize our lives.

As our sense of loss diminishes from intense sorrow to mild sadness, our appetite, sleep, energy, and functioning are restored pretty much to "normal." Similarly, we become more interested in the world and in increasing our activities.

A significant change at this time is that we are more drawn to our own future. We begin to reinvest ourselves in our life. Now we want to have a future, and we begin to get involved in creating our life ahead. We know we will not forget the one who died, but that person moves from the foreground into the background. We need to talk less often about the deceased, and we are less preoccupied with belongings, memories, and stories of the dead loved one. The loss is no less real, but our sense of impoverishment is abating. We begin to feel whole and a sense of "normality" once again.

In this reorganization phase, months after our loss, we may assume that we are recovered from our grief because we have more energy and feel more able to cope. This may not be true. Although we feel much stronger, we may still be working through our grief as intensely as before, but in more subtle, less obvious ways. This then may be a time of aftershocks in the form of unexpected jolts of upset feelings or sudden reminders of our loss and grief. For example, one young widow who felt ready to enjoy herself and even to love again went out on a date several months after her husband's death. Suddenly after one drink she found herself crying hysterically with the new man she wanted to impress. Lynn Caine in *Widow* talked about her move to the suburbs, an impulsive decision that turned out to be devastatingly unhappy for herself and her children. And an easygoing woman named Alice found herself suddenly enraged at a friend who complained about her teenage daughter, when all Alice could think of was her desolation at no longer having a daughter at all. Even though reorganization begins our re-entry and reinvestment in living, our continued internal processing of grief keeps us from feeling fully "normal" yet.

Although we are now beginning to fully let go of the deceased, this resolution does not necessarily happen spontaneously or naturally. Sometimes we need to solidify the process of letting go. We may need a context in which we let go, be it a ceremony or a set time or a planned arrangement for saying good-bye. In chapter 12, "Finishing," there are many ideas on how to accomplish the necessary resolution of grief.

Our beliefs affect our mourning. If we believe in a life after death, in heaven, or in rebirth, it often is easier to consider letting go of the deceased for now. Resolution may take longer, though, when we believe that the good-bye we must say is permanent.

Whatever our beliefs, we might try saying good-bye to the picture or memory of the deceased and imagine the loved one as floating upward into the vast universe, to help us give solid form to our good-bye. This can be a serious beginning to letting go. Acknowledging good-bye *out loud* can be particularly helpful.

Of course, there may be difficult days even after the full thrust of mourning is complete. Anniversaries or reminders may provoke grief again for a moment. The re-emergence of grief at these times is a natural part of coming to terms with accepting the death of a loved one.

The reorganization phase, like the whole experience of grief, will vary for each of us. Usually this is a time of thrusting ourselves back into the mainstream of life, reconnecting with a sense of our future, and letting go of the profound intensity of grief. More elaboration of the means to complete and to recover will be found in chapters 11 and 12.

When we do not allow ourselves to experience fully every aspect of the grieving process, we create many difficulties for ourselves. These problems will be elaborated on in the next chapter.

7

Unsuccessful Grief

And a ship without rudder may wander aimlessly
among perilous isles yet sink not to the bottom.
　　　　　　　　　　　　—The Prophet

Healthy grief, dramatic and even traumatic as it may be, is a three-stage process. First, it is fully experiencing and expressing all the emotions and reactions to the loss. Second, it is completing and letting go of your attachment both to the deceased and to sorrow. Third, it is recovering and reinvesting anew in one's own life. Missing any of the steps in the grieving process may result in unhealthy or unsuccessful grief. Because these stages may take many months, unsuccessful grief may not show up until long after the loss. However, when even unsuccessful grief becomes evident, it can be explored and successfully resolved. Unsuccessful grief is usually reversible.

For us to complete every step of the grieving process requires awareness, courage, openness, self-support, and support from others. Because of the complexity of this process, many of us do not fully complete each necessary step. That is why unsuccessful or unhealthy grief is common. Further complicating our completion of the grieving process is the fact that our responses to loss are often automatic or unconscious, so that we may be unaware of what we are going through.

Since the grieving process is mostly learned, few of us experience healthy grief without first using more unsuitable means for coping with our pain and sorrow. We are more apt to deal successfully with a death when we have learned earlier to cope with loss and separation. Each of us will probably find some of the examples of unsuccessful grief familiar. The intention here, however, is to offer understanding and guidelines for coping with eventual grief rather than chastising ourselves for earlier failures.

Of the many causes of unsuccessful grief, the most basic is our lack of knowledge about experiencing and completing the mourning process. Unaware of how to grieve successfully, we attempt to deny, delay, inhibit, or displace our feelings. Indirectly expressed or unexpressed grief is unhealthy.

The other extreme—exaggerating or prolonging our grief years beyond the actual loss—is also unhealthy. This occurs when we overidealize the deceased, or hang on to such feelings as sorrow or guilt, or fail to resume our lives fully after a loss. Many of us mistakenly believe that if we truly loved we will never finish sorrowing. We see prolonged, unresolved grieving as a statement of love rather than what it really is—pathological grief. The more mature our relationship with the deceased was, the better chance we have of healthily resolving our grief.

Unsuccessful grief is also the result of the misguided ideas of courage in our society. For example, courage is often seen as a capacity to be silent when in pain, to control tears at all costs, to function regardless of the depths of turmoil inside us, and to handle our wounds and sorrows privately and independently. Few of us are so superhuman. When we try to act according to these ideals, we usually deny our pain and never learn to cope with it. Since pain unexpressed does not dissolve spontaneously, we may suffer severe consequences from pretending to be superhuman. An extreme example of this was Anna, whose husband died unexpectedly when both were in their early sixties. From the day of his death, Anna never mentioned her husband and never shed a tear. Within a year, she had symptoms of senility. Now, several years later, Anna is completely senile, though not yet seventy years old. Another example of massive self-control was George, who seemed to face the death of his son stoically, without tears. Yet George died of a heart attack six months later.

Both Anna and George suffered terrible consequences of their enormous control over their grief feelings.

Although we may feel "crazy" or out of control when grieving, few of us actually lose our grip on reality for any extended period of time. But when we force ourselves to contain our grief or deny our loss, we may lose control over our mental faculties. This is an unhealthy state that may require psychiatric medication or hospitalization to give us the opportunity to grieve and to reorganize.

It takes enormous courage to face pain directly and honestly, to sit in the midst of such uncomfortable feelings and reactions until we have expressed them and finished with them. It takes courage to be willing to experience fully the pain and anguish of grief and to face feelings at the time they occur rather than postponing the encounter.

The most extreme form of unexpressed grief is *absent grief*. The death of a loved one is such a shock that initially we often go numb and have no reaction at all for a short time. However, to have no reaction to the death of a loved one weeks or months later can be symptomatic of pathological grief. To repress a major emotional onslaught, like grief, can wreak havoc with our emotional and physical health. The suppression of grief can incapacitate us by causing our emotions to be deadened or distorted, our relationships to suffer, and our functioning to be impaired.

A word of caution about absent grief: Sometimes we truly have no grief. This may occur when we actually resolved the relationship with the deceased prior to the death, or when we had no great emotional investment in the person who died. Some deeply spiritual people accept death immediately and positively and therefore do not grieve. And older people, who have had more experience with death, may accept a loss more readily. When a long illness preceded the loved one's death, grief may have been worked through in advance. And some people grieve in secret. Such private grieving is not to be confused with the absence of grief.

Denial of grief is similar to absent grief. Overwhelmed by a loss, we try to postpone facing the fact of death. Some denial is natural in the process of getting used to the loss, but denial as one's only mechanism for coping is unhealthy.

Denial of grief usually appears in the guise of pretending not to feel rather than in a true absence of feelings. For example, a child's announcement that he feels nothing, when clearly he is moody, negative, or withdrawn, indicates a denied reaction. Adults sometimes act the same way, or they may become very busy to cover up grief. Denial may be a fragile defense, which another can break through with openness and kindly encouragement.

Grief is inhibited when the bereaved, or someone close, shuts off the natural flow of feelings about the loss. Fear of the feelings or their intensity, discomfort with tears and false pride about silence and self-control are all things that inhibit grief. We are bound to be inhibited in our grief and unable to complete it if we cannot express our feelings. Silence or the "stiff upper lip" approach to grief causes inner turmoil and eventual problems. Grief feelings linger and emerge in some other way later on.

Delayed grief is the pushing aside of feelings at the critical early stages of mourning to be dealt with at some future time. Often we lack the courage to confront grief feelings at their strongest, and we imagine that delaying grief will make it easier later on. Sometimes, too, we delay in order to maintain our functioning or to assist someone else who is grieving at the same time. Whether the impetus to delay grief is conscious or unconscious, delayed grief is simply bottled-up pain that will erupt with its original force at some later time or in some other area of our lives. Delaying grief always leaves us open to an unexpected emotional explosion.

There are many signs of unsuccessful or inhibited grief. Sudden personality changes and progressive social isolation after a loss may signify unresolved grief. The bereaved may become apathetic or unusually contained and careful. In controlling their feelings, especially unresolved hostility, the bereaved may become "wooden and formal." There may be a refusal to talk about the deceased or to even mention his or her name. Similarly, emotionally loaded topics of conversation are apt to be avoided. The inhibited survivor may fail to acknowledge feelings or may always face grief from an intellectual rather than an emotional perspective. Death may be referred to casually or not at all. Nonverbal clues of inhibited grief are obvious body tension, stiff posture, taut neck, tense or brittle smile, lack of eye contact, tense gesturing such as pacing or finger-tapping, or withdrawn behavior.

Whether we are aware of it or not, we pay an enormous price for inhibiting grief. Sometimes the price is a loss of our zest for living that may continue for months or even years. After we suffer a loss that we have not fully mourned, we may withdraw from others or decide that closeness is not worth the effort. We may simply get into a life pattern of overworking in order to maintain our avoidance. Others of us will need several drinks to get through the day or will rely on drugs or medication. Promiscuity, excessive gambling, and other compulsive behaviors may be covers for unresolved grief. Constant colds or other chronic physical symptoms may be the price we pay for inhibiting our grief. Preoccupation with death or suicide is another possible sign of unexpressed grief.

Many experiences can trigger the grief that was earlier avoided. These might include another loss, another kind of upset in our life, a new experience like the birth of a child, the reappearance of an old friend or an old memory, a movie, a book, and especially an important anniversary or date in our own life or in that of the deceased. "Anniversary reactions"—one or even fifty years after a death—are common for most of us, whether we have fully grieved or not. Anniversaries are all the more potent when our feelings about the loss were suppressed. We may be caught by surprise at a time that may feel inappropriate, or when there is no support from others. These are times when most of us need some help in completing the grieving process; usually this help can come from some professional.

In my experience the majority of clients come for psychotherapy for the first time because of an earlier grief that is now affecting their lives. It has been a profound experience to see how frequently the precipitant of the current problem was an earlier unresolved loss. Many times typical life incidents such as a graduation, marriage, or the birth of a child bring forth grief for a dead parent, grandparent, or sibling who was not only missing the event but perhaps had never had the opportunity for the same experience. Other traumas such as a car accident, an illness, or the loss of a job can precipitate unresolved grief.

Whenever grief is discovered as unresolved, it is time to deal with it, for it is never too late to express the grief and complete the grieving process. Usually the problem arises because the survivor had to face the feelings of grief alone in the first place, so clearly the bereaved now should not try to go it alone. A professional counselor or therapist who can help us come to terms with the loss and whatever feelings are unresolved should be sought out. Chapter 12, "Finishing," is also designed to help with the completion of grief.

Exaggerated grief, or chronic bereavement—the opposite of unexpressed grief—is also unhealthy. This is grief that remains prominent in our lives years beyond the loss. Significant here is how long the grief has persisted. Other symptoms are morbid brooding and continued striving for reunion with the deceased well after the death occurs. Similarly, being preoccupied too long with the dead loved one rather than redefining goals and reinvesting in our lives is pathological behavior. Some other clues to chronic grief are talking about the deceased in the present tense, as if he or she is alive, and overvaluing objects and ideas that belonged to the deceased.

Excessive bereavement is usually tolerated by bystanders because continuing sorrow is often so moving. We tend to romanticize prolonged grief instead of seeing it as pathological. We also tolerate such grief because we do not know what to do to encourage someone to complete the grieving process.

Something important is missing in the grieving process of a person who cannot come to some resolution of a death after many years. It is unhealthy for a survivor to cling to a loss; eventually he or she must let go. Hidden feelings, too painful to face, are often the underlying cause of prolonged grief. Any feelings could fall in this category, but most of us find it particularly hard to tolerate our ambivalence, resentment, and guilt toward a loved one who dies. Therefore, we continue living amid the intensity of our sorrow in order to block off the other unacceptable feelings. At times, we prolong grief because of our extreme dependency on the deceased, hanging on to avoid taking new, independent action in our lives. Sometimes our fears of life are harder to face than our grief, which by now is familiar. Fear of new relationships, of sexuality, of responsibility, and of change may keep us from completing the grieving process. Finally, when grief has brought us more support and attention from others than we ever before received, it may be painfully difficult to let go of the special treatment afforded us as the bereaved.

Hanging on to any particular memory, feeling, or idea years after a loss is also unhealthy. Since life naturally involves continual change, clinging to the past impedes our growth. For example, Bill is a man who, twenty years after his son died, continues to regret that he did not assist him in choosing a different college. This process of reviewing and rewriting history years later is a form of hanging on to the past and indicates unsuccessful grieving. Like all the other symptoms of mourning, obsessive thinking about the deceased is characteristic of the first months of grieving and is pathological when it persists years beyond the normal mourning period.

Guilt is one of the most prominent and uncomfortable feelings that interferes with the successful completion of grief. So often we are unwilling to forgive ourselves years beyond whatever error we committed, or even when we are blameless. Our lack of self-forgiveness perpetuates the grieving process. For example, parents tend to feel overly responsible for a child who dies, regardless of the circumstances, and to blame themselves unjustly, as if they had been somehow negligent.

Likewise, clinging to an unfulfilled promise made by the deceased indicates a lack of resolution of grief. For example, Edna, whose husband died leaving her with young children, resented for years that he had betrayed his promise to help raise their two sons. Similarly, many a client of mine has blamed some earlier loss in life for his or her lack of later success, continuing to cling to such ideas as "If only he had lived, my life would have worked" or "I would be happy" or "I would have enough self-confidence now." Whenever "if onlys" persist years beyond a loss, grief is clearly unresolved. Professional help is probably in order, because we are likely to be unwilling to face alone the necessary grief work ahead.

Overidealization of the deceased that persists after the first year or so of mourning is usually symptomatic of unsuccessful grief. In many cases, the one we loved becomes all the more wonderful once we are parted. Without the loved one's presence in our daily lives, we can forget those things that irritated or annoyed us. Focusing only on the positive and idealizing the loved one also enables us to deny uncomfortable feelings like resentment, ambivalence, and guilt. Overidealization may also indicate our unwillingness to return to reality. However, romanticizing the deceased actually creates more problems for us by making reality look all the more empty in comparison with the idealized past.

Emily was a woman who literally created a shrine to her deceased husband, which consisted of photographs and other memorabilia. When guests came, she acted as if she expected them to join in worship at the shrine. Most ironic was the fact that her deceased husband had been a somewhat shady businessman, quite a contrast to the god she created when he died.

er woman, Nora, changed her physician husband Arthur
lint after his death. Although Arthur had been an outstanding and beloved man, he was also bad-tempered, overly
demanding, and intolerant. Nora's children became bitter when
their mother made their father into a mythological figure whom
they could no longer remember realistically. Nora's denial of what
her husband was really like made it hard for the whole family
to resolve the loss, so intense was Nora in "selling" the new
image of Arthur. Nora's family saw her pathological idealization
of Arthur as a way to glorify herself, for she was clearly a woman
for whom going on alone, no longer the partner of a successful
man, was a lonely and frightening prospect.

In addition to exaggerated and underexpressed grief, there are
symptoms that point up unsuccessful grief, the most prominent
of which are fearfulness, anxiety, depression, and psychosomatic
symptoms. Because depression and grief seem similar, it is important to be able to distinguish between the two. In both, one is
apt to experience loss of appetite, weight loss, insomnia, lack
of sexual interest, and self-blame. However, when these symptoms persist beyond a year of mourning the chances are that
the person is now depressed. Grief eventually lifts, while depression often seems to become persistently worse. Instead of being
preoccupied with the deceased, the depressed individual tends
to be more preoccupied with self, blaming self and relating to
self as "bad" rather than bereaved. Freud delineated depression
or melancholia by the extreme diminishing of self-regard. We
tend to be sympathetic to one who is grieving, and more irritated
with one who is depressed, so obsessive is his or her negativity.
The person grieving will often respond, relate, and even laugh
at times, while the depressed person is usually humorless and
unresponsive. Psychological therapy and sometimes antidepres-
sant medication are ways to help resolve depression.

Anxiety or fearfulness that persists much beyond the loss experience is another sign of unsuccessful grief. General tenseness,
difficulty in concentrating, stage fright, sweatiness without or-

ganic basis, facial flushing, and heart palpitations are symptoms of anxiety. Death and loss can shake us to our very core. If we do not allow deep feelings to emerge while grieving, our bottled-up feelings may make us tense or nervous. Sometimes our anxiety is a way of anticipating life after a loss. Unexpected deaths especially catch us off guard, leaving us feeling vulnerable and helpless. After such a loss we sometimes put ourselves on guard, consciously or not, as if we could fend off future assaults on our emotions.

Fearfulness is a more exaggerated form of anxiety. Fear of the loss of other loved ones is common after we suffer one loss. We may find ourselves obsessively watching every move a surviving child or a spouse makes. We are terrified that the trauma will be repeated. Trying to stifle our fears often makes them worse, creating a vicious cycle. Again, a professional counselor can help us break through fears and resolve the persisting grief that lies behind them.

Sometimes we are unaware of a connection between our fears and our unresolved grief. Such was the case of Helen, a former client of mine. Helen had a chronic fear of traveling. She was afraid to leave her house and did so only to attend her twice-weekly clinic appointments for therapy. She refused to travel by car, so she would walk the many blocks to the clinic. When we began together, she had had several years of unsuccessful therapy with a long line of therapists. To me, the most significant thing in Helen's background was that she had been on an exciting automobile trip throughout the United States when her mother unexpectedly died. Because Helen was out of reach, traveling without a planned itinerary, she did not hear the news until after the funeral. Not only had Helen been unable to be with her mother when she died, she had also missed the funeral and sharing the loss with the rest of her family. Helen was consumed with guilt and regret that she had been traveling and having fun when her mother may have needed her. The root of Helen's travel phobia is obvious. She decided unconsciously that as a protection against further disasters in her life and as a punishment for herself, she would never travel again. Helen's guilt was compounded by ambivalent feelings about her mother, feelings that are typical of most of us. Hence, it was hard for her to relinquish her guilt. But once she fully accepted her feelings and managed to forgive herself, her travel phobia disappeared.

Helen's reaction may seem childish to some of us, but it shows that a traumatic loss in our lives can provoke our most primitive reactions. Suppressing these can create a neurotic symptom, like Helen's, or anxiety or depression or a physical symptom. To avoid such reactions, we need to express our feelings openly rather than suppress them.

Fear of death is an obvious and common symptom of unresolved grief. Anita was thirteen when her mother died of cancer. Because Anita had not been told of her mother's impending death, she developed a terror of facing unexpected death that persisted for years. Anita was afraid to close her eyes at night, lest she not wake up. She was afraid she would be injured or killed if she attempted to take part in sports or other physical activities. She was afraid to ride in cars, and she never ventured into an airplane. She watched her body attentively for any signs of a life-threatening illness, like that of her mother's. So obsessed was Anita with fears of her own demise that she was less and less able to function or even to venture out of her home. Fortunately a school counselor sensed Anita's need for help. As Anita eventually resolved her shock and grief, her symptoms and fears disappeared.

Hypochondria, like fears of death, is typical during mourning and pathological when carried beyond the confines of the initial grieving period. Anxiety about one's health without real basis, or creating imaginary illnesses, is characteristic of the hypochondriac. For example, in someone preoccupied with illness and death, a headache might signal a brain tumor or a gas pain might set off fear of a heart attack. Imitating the illness suffered by the deceased is common. For example, if the loved one died of cancer, the survivor may imagine or become preoccupied with symptoms that might possibly indicate cancer. For many of us it is easier to pay attention to physical rather than emotional distress. We also may be more at ease in enlisting another's help for physical rather than emotional problems. Sometimes the stress of grief provokes real physical problems in the bereaved, or it may aggravate a pre-existing physical or emotional problem. In an important psychological study, Erich Lindemann's concern was that in avoiding the pain of grief one might develop illnesses such as asthma, migraines, colitis, and arthritis, as well as emotional disorders. Therefore, whether symptoms seem real or imaginary, it is a good idea to consult a physician to be sure.

Grief can become somaticized and turn into a real physical illness. Disease then acts as a substitute for the unresolved sorrow. The loss of a loved one, if not successfully grieved and resolved, can precipitate a serious, even life-threatening, illness. Psychiatrist David Peretz notes, "It has been postulated that depression and/or marked feelings of helplessness lower resistance to infection and perhaps even reduce the body's immune defense." Carl and Stephanie Simonton, innovative researchers on the subject of psychological factors in cancer, concur, noting that high levels of stress and chronic stress—which is what unresolved grief becomes—leave one more susceptible to illness.

In summary, the best solution for unsuccessful grief, whenever and however it is discovered, is to resolve the grief as fully as possible. Emotional honesty can be instrumental here. What is not easy is that in order to resolve grief, feelings need to be re-experienced anew, and each step of the mourning process must be completed. This may be too difficult for someone to tackle alone. However, clues to enable us to finish with grief are discussed in detail in chapter 12. Otherwise, the grieving person should seek professional help. Most psychotherapists are trained to uncover unresolved grief, and many have special skills for resolution. Guidelines for choosing a therapist are found in chapter 10, "Helping Ourselves with Grief."

Loss can precipitate a wide range of psychological and physical problems. Since grief and unresolved grief are such pervasive human problems, we need to be understanding, tolerant, and aware of the difficulties each of us has in completing the grieving process. We must also remember that whenever grief is uncovered it can be resolved successfully.

Up to now, emphasis has been on the adult mourning experience. But, children also grieve. Children's grief is the subject of the next chapter.

8

Children's Grief

Your children are not your children.
They are the sons and daughters of Life's longing for itself.
They come through you but not from you.
And though they are with you yet they belong not to you.

You may give them your love but not your thoughts,
For they have their own thoughts.

—The Prophet

Educator and author Eda LeShan notes, "A child can live through *anything,* so long as he or she is told the truth and is allowed to share with loved ones the natural feelings people have when they are suffering." For most of us, however, confronting the unpleasant reality of death with a child seems an unbearable task. Our own fears of death and the denial of death, so prevalent in our society, make it excruciatingly difficult to face death honestly and directly with children. Hence, out of our own inhibitions we often deprive children of the chance to begin to grapple with their loss and their ideas about death.

Our attitudes toward children also deter us from sharing openly and honestly with them. Because we have difficulty understanding and accepting death, we often convince ourselves that death is beyond the grasp of children. On the one hand, we seem to deny that children are feeling, potentially suffering human beings, and we imagine instead that they are too undeveloped to experience real grief. On the other hand, we fear how deeply children will suffer from a loss, and we want to spare or protect them from the suffering of grief. Similarly, we do not want to frighten or overwhelm them with our tears. They may be scared of tears, but they will recover more easily if told the truth. Even if the facts of a death are not shared, children invariably know the truth, or at least sense trouble. They then suffer all the more in isolation.

The seeming limitations of children further inhibit us from facing death with them. We may avoid attempting serious communication with them, because they are characteristically unable to communicate in an adult manner. We may become impatient with them for their failure to share their feelings, or we may even come to believe that, when feelings remain unexpressed, none exist. Of course, children's limited vocabularies and sometimes inhibited responses to feelings *can* interfere with intimate discussions. Some children, however, are so disarmingly honest about their feelings that they provoke anxiety in adults who are not as open. When children can express deep feelings, it shows that they are emotionally healthy.

Although children have many of the same feelings adults do, their outward display is often more confused or defensive. Children's defensive responses to loss can be irritating or anxiety-producing for adults, who then shy away from sharing their own emotions. When confronted with the fact of death, children may respond defensively. For example, they may say things like "Bang, bang, you're dead" or "I don't love him anyway," or laugh anxiously. At first they may change the subject, run off to play, express resentment that their activities are suddenly curtailed, or seem to have no particular reaction to the news of a death. Adults can help a child with grief and death by giving less weight to the child's attitude and by continuing to be open, honest, and kind, regardless of the child's behavior. Unfortunately, empathy between parents and children is often disrupted in situations of stress.

When a death occurs, children should be told the truth immediately in a loving, natural way, preferably by a parent or by someone very close to them. The words and explanations about death need to be simple, direct, and honest. We can share our own beliefs, doubts, and questions. By avoiding issues and feelings, we fail our children. Euphemisms, such as saying a dead loved one has "gone away on vacation," cloud and deny reality.

Likewise, sending children away from the family or away from the situation of grief, or ignoring their bereavement, shows disrespect for their feelings and denies them their rightful grief. Being sent away may seem to a child like a terrible punishment, and it will intensify the already growing sense of anguish.

Grief is complicated for children because the fear of separation from their parents is so prominent. Loss can seem to threaten a child's very survival. Absence of a parent can provoke severe anxiety in young children, for without someone to meet their physical and emotional needs their life seems to be in danger. Therefore, children need reassurance that they will not be left alone and that their needs will be met. As children grow older and develop more independence in their skills and relationships outside the family, separation anxieties diminish. Fear of separation is an issue for each of us until our independence and individuality are clearly established.

Although the signs of grief in children may be less obvious than in adults, children do grieve. Their reactions of grief are complicated by their often unconscious attempts to mask feelings and by their defensive behavior. Children may react defensively to the news of a death by denial, blandness, brazenness, even joking, any of which may dismay or anger the adults around them. Children may cling to daydreams that deny the reality. The less they understand, the more likely they are to be apprehensive and fearful. They may become afraid that another loved one will die, and they may literally cling to that other person, or they may fear their own death. Their sadness may be intermittent or short-lived. An important difference between grieving adults and grieving children is that children usually do not sustain sadness over long periods of time.

Children may not be able to share their reactions to a death verbally. Sometimes children may be able to express themselves more easily by telling a story or drawing pictures of their experiences. Sharing their feelings through stories or drawings can be a meaningful way for upset or grieving children to release their emotions. We should always be aware that children can sense when adults do not want them to share their feelings. When children are closed off in this way, a destructive pattern of swallowing their feelings to please others often results.

Significant, too, when children do not reveal their feelings is their concern for those around them. "Often a child is unable to express what he is feeling to his parents because the parents, too, may be upset by whatever happened, and the child feels protective toward them; he doesn't want to cause them any more grief and unhappiness. If the parents can face their own feelings openly, the child can more easily be open with his own feelings and confusions."

Reactions to death differ according to a child's age or stage of development. Psychologist Maria Nagy notes the following developmental differences in children's reactions to death. From ages three to five, children tend to see death as akin to sleep or a journey, from which one can wake up or return. The permanence of death is not yet realized. From five to nine years of age, children understand the reality of death, but they have difficulty imagining that they or their loved ones will die. At nine or ten, children realize the irreversible nature of death. At the same time, they are more curious about its biological aspects, and they are aware of the social implications of death and loss for the survivors. Adolescents may regress to earlier concepts of death, but usually they become preoccupied, as do adults, with a search for the meaning of death.

Children have the hardest time accepting death when they have had the least preparation for loss and death. It is hard for us to prepare for the sudden loss of a loved one. However, we can begin to prepare a child for death itself long before death has to be faced. Instead of avoiding the issue of death with children, acknowledging death as an everyday reality is a kind of preparation. Most children see death early in life, be it a dead insect, bird, squirrel, or personal pet. Usually less charged, these deaths offer an opportunity for children and adults to consider together the questions that are bound to arise for every child about death, whether the child verbalizes them or not. A child's questions may be: What is death? Why do we die? Will I die? Will you die? What happens after death? When concepts are not explained to them truthfully, children tend to scare themselves and imagine the worst. Exploring these questions before a major loss occurs not only helps the child examine death but also gives parents a chance to confront difficult questions without having to cope with anxiety and grief at the same time. However, parents may need to expand their own understanding of death in order to be able to help the child.

Most important, parents can help a child accept death by treating death as a natural reality, noticing death and commenting on it spontaneously. If the opportunity arises, parents and children might bury a dead animal together. This might provoke the child to examine different concepts of death. As a child, my unsuccessful attempts to dig up a dead canary long after I had buried it led to my conceding that death was permanent.

Handling death with children will depend on whether the death is sudden or follows a protracted illness. Children, like adults, suffer shock and denial when first hearing of a loss. Advance preparation lessens the sense of shock and enables them to cope more easily with the loss. Children should not be shielded from the dying process of a loved one. Shielding children from dying denies them the opportunity to continue to relate to the dying loved one and intensifies the shock when death does occur. So many of my clients still suffered as adults the pain of unexpected, unprepared-for death of a loved parent or grandparent because as children they were overly protected from illness and death.

Sharing the dying process can be a special and rewarding experience for both. A loving child can give great support to the person who is dying. Having the opportunity to share with a dying loved one also helps children learn about death in a natural way; they get to share their feelings with the loved one, and otherwise-unfinished business can be completed before the death occurs. Even though children may seem to deny that a loved one is dying, or have difficulty in forming a concept of death, when the truth is shared they have a greater chance to grieve fully and accept the loss.

When we shield children from death there may be serious consequences. Children suffer deeply from silence as well as from evasion, denial, and fictions about death. Overly protected children can be terrorized by death. For example, Tim, who was twelve, suffered from severe fears of illness and death for several years after his mother died. Although his mother was sick for several months prior to her death, Tim was told that his mother was recovering. Tim's shock, his sense of loss, and his anger at his father for shielding him from death left him bereft and emotionally upset throughout adolescence. In contrast, Carol knew all the details of her father's illness and death. As an adult, Carol feels she grasped the reality and resolved the loss then in her childhood. Similarly, when Rita's husband died of a heart attack, she let her sons, ages five and seven, see their father. The three shared their feelings openly together. Both boys seemed to grasp and accept the death in a matter of months, much more quickly, in fact, than their mother did.

Children's grief can be easily inhibited. Sometimes children feel ashamed to cry. They are also inhibited by misguided adults who encourage them to "Be brave" or "Be a little man" or "Be a good, quiet girl" or "Don't be a crybaby." Children often respond obediently to these injunctions and stifle their own grief to their detriment. As I said earlier, grieving is learned behavior. Adults can support and assist a child to grieve fully to completion, or adults can limit a child's ability to grieve by their words or injunctions and by the behavior they offer the child to imitate. Both words and actions teach children about grief, as about other experiences in life. An excellent book for children that clarifies and supports grief is Eda LeShan's *Learning to Say Good-by*.

John Bowlby, the noted psychiatrist and expert on loss and separation in children, describes three phases of children's grief that are very similar to the three phases of adult mourning. He calls the first phase the protest phase, where the child denies and resists the idea of death and loss. The second phase is the disorganization phase, during which the child eventually acknowledges that the lost loved one will not return. The third phase for both children and adults is the reorganization phase, when acceptance of the loss and letting go of the deceased begin to occur. At this time children reinvest more in their lives and yet may be subject to upsets related to grief. Children grieve for a shorter time span than adults, unless their grief is severely inhibited or interfered with.

Physician George E. Williams, in the eighth of a fifteen-part newspaper course on death and dying sponsored by the University of California, San Diego, discussed five phases of children's grief that coincide with Kübler-Ross's five stages of grief in facing one's own death. The first phase of grief is denial or isolation. The second phase is anger. (Unlike adults, children may be more openly angry in response to a loss. For example, children may suddenly and unaccountably become angry at a surviving parent or sibling, or they may be openly hostile to the deceased.) The third phase is the bargaining phase, where children try to change the reality of death, for example, by promising, "I'll be good." The fourth phase, depression, is when the children's anger is turned back on themselves. While mourning, children, like adults, may experience symptoms such as nightmares or other sleep difficulties, appetite or weight loss, or physical aches and pains. The resolution phase, the final phase of mourning, is when a child finally accepts the loved one's death.

Guilt can be a particular problem for children facing a loss. Children may take the loss personally and blame themselves for some previous "bad" behavior, or perhaps for their ambivalent feelings toward the deceased. The loss of a parent is always complicated by the child's ambivalence toward that parent. Because parenting involves frequently frustrating children, it is natural that children at times hate the parent and even wish the parent dead. If the parent dies, children may feel guilt and fear that they caused the death. This guilt can be counteracted by understanding adults who kindly reassure a child that he or she is blameless.

Signs of regression may appear in the behavior of grieving children. After a loss, children may revert to earlier problem behaviors, such as bed-wetting, temper tantrums, thumbsucking, or clinging to adults. This regression, however, is usually temporary. Again, allowing full expression of grief will keep these symptoms from persisting.

Any sudden personality changes may indicate that children are unsuccessful in their grieving. Unsuccessful grief in children is characterized by extreme denial or by morbid brooding over the loss months after the death occurs. A child who is obsessively preoccupied with fantasies of reunion, or a child who months later refuses to admit that a loved one is actually dead, is unsuccessfully coping with grief. Extensive depression, a symptom that indicates internal suffering, should be taken seriously when it occurs in children. Symptoms of depression in children might be persistent withdrawal, listlessness, recurring psychosomatic stomachaches or headaches, nightmares, or losing friends through either aggressiveness or withdrawal.

Children heal much more quickly than adults. One open, honest, loving conversation with children about death can often help them move toward resolving their grief. When facing grief with children is too hard for parents to do, another loving adult can help. If another adult friend or relative is unavailable, a rabbi, minister, priest, understanding teacher, or professional counselor specializing in children's problems can help children complete their grief.

The grief reactions of adolescents are similar to those of adults and children. Because adolescents typically regress under a severe stress such as a loss, their reactions may be more like those of children. However, there are specific issues of adolescent grief that affect their reactions. Adolescence is a time rich in fantasy. Adolescents in mourning may become preoccupied with rewriting the reality of the death with daydreams that deny or delay their grief. Another complicating factor is the adolescent's struggle between independence and dependence. Death can be particularly threatening for adolescents, who may develop fears of separation and independence. Because teenagers often appear more mature, or mask their feelings better than children do, their grief feelings can become unhealthily buried. Finally, adolescents are unique in their self-consciousness. They may seem to be more preoccupied with their behavior or their clothes than with the loss itself, a perfect means of denial that is nonetheless confusing and irritating to those around them.

Children and adolescents alike have many needs during mourning, the most important of which is their need for love, support, and companionship. They need to express their feelings and ask questions. Often they cannot take additional pressure, even when they appear to be reacting calmly. Any demand on a child to behave in a new way may be met with resistance. For example, suddenly to have to be quiet, or to be open about feelings, may be too hard for the child. Likewise, expecting children to fulfill new roles—for example, to take over for a deceased parent or sibling—may frighten them and accentuate their grief. As with any mourner, children need to be respected for being what they are and not be expected to change suddenly.

Because of their own distress, grieving parents may not be able to be with their children immediately after sustaining a loss. Rather than pushing the children off to the side or sending them away, this can be explained to them by another supportive adult. For example, the adult might simply say, "Mom is too upset right now to be with you. She needs to be by herself to cry, so she asked me to spend this afternoon with you. Perhaps you need to cry too." Parents' honest responses to grief are the best way to teach a child how to grieve. Candid responses and permission for the child to respond truthfully are the most helpful tools for grieving.

Children of all ages should be encouraged to participate in whatever rituals, customs, or forms of grieving there are in the family, if the children wish to be involved. These are opportunities for learning about death, as well as times of family cohesiveness. However, children should never be forced to join in any mourning practices against their will, no matter how good the adults may think the experience may be for them. Certain rituals, such as kissing the dead body of a loved one, may seem primitive and frightening to a child. Other rituals, however, such as viewing the body of the deceased in an open casket, may enable the child as well as the adult to confront death more realistically. When we are unsure how to proceed, we should describe the process ahead to the children and ask if they want to participate.

To summarize, helping children with grief, like helping adults, involves honesty, kindness, and acceptance of the child's reactions and behavior. Though children may react defensively, they still grieve and need much support to go through the grieving process to completion. When they are helped with their grief, children tend to heal more quickly than adults.

PART THREE

The Recovery Process

9

Helping Others with Grief

You give but little when you give of
your possessions. It is when you give
of yourself that you truly give.
　　　　　—The Prophet

Confronting loss and death is hard for us survivors. We feel overwhelmed and helpless when we hear of another's loss. One conse-
quence of the denial of death in our society is that we are often
ignorant and unskilled in coping with loss, be it our own or another's. We may want to help, but we don't know how. Having
no idea what to do when we hear of a death, many of us run
away from helping the bereaved. However, there are a number
of ways we can help others in grief.

A grieving friend needs our friendship and support to go
through and complete the mourning process. We must reach out
and take the initiative in offering help. The most valuable thing
we have to give is our presence. It is far more important than
our knowledge or our advice, for the companionship of family
and friends is the greatest source of support and solace. We can
help our grieving friend most by sitting near, holding a hand,
giving a hug, passing a tissue, crying together, listening, sharing
our feelings. In other words, what the bereaved need most is
our acknowledgment of their pain and sorrow. And we both must
realize that we cannot erase that pain. In coping with loss, the
bereaved are greatly depleted of energy. The presence of others
helps energize and renew them. Sometimes mourners feel a drop
in energy when guests depart, as if it is other people who almost
literally hold them up.

Often we imagine there is a "right" way to act, if only we knew what the right way was. Many of us struggle to find exactly the right words, when a simple "I'm sorry" is enough. Though some words may offer solace, there are few "right" words for the occasion of grief. Being a caring presence and a good listener is more important than any words we might say. Above all, the bereaved need loving people to stand by them through their suffering. This is truly what support is all about. Not having to suffer alone is often the greatest gift we can offer the bereaved. Alone is harder. Alone is when fear and anguish are overwhelming. Alone accentuates the despair and emptiness of loss.

When helping others who are grieving, we need to realize that people have different needs during the different phases of grief. In the initial period of shock, practical help is often most needed, while emotional understanding may not yet reach the bereaved. However, emotional support is critical during the suffering period of grief. Our sensitivity to a grieving friend's needs might be enhanced by reviewing the information on the grief experience in parts One and Two.

When we do not know what to do for another person, a good rule of thumb is to ask ourselves, "What would I like done for me under these circumstances?" Another good rule is to sense— or ask directly about—the mourner's needs. For example, if the bereaved needs to talk, then by all means we should respond. If the other wants quiet, we should be quiet too, and not rush to fill the silence. And we must remember to focus on giving, not on taking. The bereaved person needs much help and rarely has much to give in return. If we are in need ourselves, we should stay away, so we won't place an additional strain on the mourner.

Practical assistance to those grieving is also of great value. For example, considerate people who bring a casserole for dinner and leave are as appreciated as those who stay around for many hours. What ordinarily are simple tasks can be extremely hard for the bereaved to handle. Answering the phone, screening phone calls or callers, getting groceries, doing errands, cleaning up the dishes or the house, listing who wrote or brought gifts, and answering sympathy notes—all these are necessary tasks that usually go beyond the capacities of those in mourning.

There are many other difficult tasks involved with death that those in mourning usually cannot fully handle alone. The help of friends is an enormous relief in dealing with such decisions as the disposition of the body or the belongings of the deceased, or notifying people who must be told. The organization of people in the background, behind a grieving family, is a powerful help at the time of a loss. Appendix B, in the back of this book, lists details that need to be taken care of when a death occurs.

Mourners should be spared from making decisions they are not ready to make. We can help by not pressing them about the future. We need to keep a check on our own anxieties that may compel us to question or to give advice. If decisions must be made, we may have to contribute our best judgment. Whenever possible, decisions that leave room for a change of heart are best. We may also help a grieving friend delay an impulsive or unreasonable decision.

The bereaved often need a special friend to act as a kind of spokesperson or intermediary. This person can also act as a confidant, as well as someone who can comfortably run interference for the grieving family. Such an intermediary needs to be comfortable protecting the bereaved, even if it means being impolite at times. When the family members seem overtired, the intermediary may screen phone calls or visitors or take responsibility for asking guests to leave. It is a great help to have a friend or friends who can offer this specialized kind of help.

In order to be a truly helpful friend to the bereaved, we need to decide whether we can tolerate the other's pain or not. It is extremely painful to be a witness to intense mourning. It is tempting, when uncomfortable because others are in the throes of grief, to shut them off, to encourage them to stop crying, to deny their pain, or to try to rush them through the painful mourning process. However, fully grieving is necessary and healthy. Denying another the opportunity to grieve fully is a great interference as well as a rejection.

If we cannot tolerate the other person's grief, then it is wrong for us to put ourselves through the ordeal. Instead, we can assist from afar by telephoning or doing errands or whatever needs to be done away from the home of the bereaved. When my brother died, my close friend shoveled snow from our sidewalk for the visitors but never came inside our house.

If we are able to tolerate the intensity of grief feelings and to let go of our self-consciousness about doing the "right" things, there is much we can give the bereaved. Tolerating another's tears is a very meaningful gift. So is listening without judging. Sometimes this means listening to the same thoughts repeated over and over. Yet that, too, is an important gift. And if we are not sure what our role should be when the other is crying, we can simply pass the tissues!

A touching story in this regard concerns a young woman named Connie, whose little boy died unexpectedly a few months before Christmas. Connie was in a department store when she became transfixed watching children one by one sit on the lap of the store Santa Claus. Her grief erupted as she watched. The Santa Claus saw her, motioned her over to him, and encouraged her to sit on his lap, asking her, "And what do you want from Santa, young lady?" Connie told Santa about her little boy's death and Santa comforted her.

It may help the bereaved to hear of our own experiences with loss. Our sharing can lift some of the painful aloneness felt by the bereaved and may contribute useful information as well. Others who have grieved can offer hope and a model for survival. However, some kinds of sharing may be disturbing or frightening to the newly bereaved, who are just trying to come to grips with loss and death. Thus, we should use judgment in sharing our experiences, knowing that we are talking to a very vulnerable human being whose needs at the moment are great.

"Don't cry!" is a cruel injunction for the bereaved, who have so few options for expressing the intense feelings of grief. Crying is essential, but it can provoke and sometimes scare those who hear it. Our underlying feelings about crying might be:

If you cry, I might cry.

If you cry, I might know I too am in pain.

If you cry, I might feel self-conscious about my own difficulty in crying.

If you cry, I might have to face the unpleasantness in my/your life.

If you cry, I might not be able to maintain my pose of strength (or dignity, or composure, or whatever).

If you cry, I might cry for all the pain in my own life and never stop crying.

Therefore, if you cry, I will have to run away or shut you up to save myself.

Similarly, such injunctions as "Buck up!" or "Cheer up!" are inappropriate. They are not only disconcerting but also rejecting.

We also deny the bereaved the right to their grief when we encourage them to avoid aspects of death and dying that might help them acknowledge the reality of death and come to terms with it. Trying to shield the bereaved from those facts of death that they want to know is unfair and delays their working through the loss. An example of this occurred when Jane, a twenty-eight-year-old woman, was prevented by her aunt from seeing her mother's body. Jane was enraged, and her grief was compounded by this deprivation. Such so-called helpers can be destructive. Likewise, pretense, avoidance, denial, or any prevention of normal grief experiences can create more emotional problems for the bereaved. It is usually best to let people know that a loved one is dying or dead and to support their involvement in the funeral, burial, and other details of the death. For most people, such involvement is a key factor in their accepting the loss and working it through. However, no one should ever be forced to participate.

Another way we deny the bereaved the right to their pain is

when we encourage the removal of possessions or reminders of the deceased. Sometimes we think that getting rid of belongings and mementos will get rid of the pain of the loss, which of course is untrue. To have no reminders of a loved one can cause even greater pain and anxiety, for it makes the dead person seem unreal and inaccessible.

People in the throes of grief are extremely sensitive to others around them. They usually know who can stand their pain and who cannot. Often it is those who have also suffered a loss— those who know and understand suffering—who offer the most solace. Mourners have a self-protective intuition about *who* will tolerate their pain with them. Conversely, mourners who are unwilling to experience their suffering will most likely gravitate toward supporters who encourage their denial.

Ways to support the bereaved vary and depend on the mourner. People who become incapacitated while grieving need help on every level. Others need to continue to function in order to testify to their capacity to cope with the loss. Both are normal responses, and we need to be sensitive to the individual style of the person grieving. We should give our support without taking over so much that the bereaved one feels incapacitated and without trying to rescue the other from facing grief feelings. We should also invite the bereaved to take part in social occasions, invitations they can freely accept or refuse.

It is important to be sensitive about how long we remain when visiting people in mourning. In not knowing what to do, visitors sometimes stay too long, waiting for cues as to when to leave. A person in mourning, grateful for our acknowledgment, may not be comfortable about asking us to leave.

Our acknowledgment of the loss is meaningful to the bereaved. That we care can be said simply and directly in person. If we do not feel intimate, or if we are uncomfortable confronting grief, we do not have to visit directly. A letter or phone call will be appreciated. A personal note, no matter how brief, is often more solace than a formal greeting card. Other ways of expressing our condolences are sending flowers or donating to a charity in memory of the deceased.

The most meaningful gifts that people gave to me when my brother died were their sharing of memories. Adding another's anecdotes to my own recollections expanded the wealth of my memories of my brother. Each recollection added new dimensions or pictures of my brother and let me know he was as important to others as he was to me. Now, when I write a condolence letter or visit the bereaved, I try to share my experience of the deceased, to give the kind of vignette I myself cherished. In other words, a meaningful condolence letter might describe an incident or aspect of the deceased, to make him or her live once again in the eyes of the survivors.

It also may be helpful to collect important mementos of the deceased, to be compiled in a scrapbook or photograph album. Keepsakes like photographs, clippings, even stories about the deceased can provide a satisfying memorial later on. We often fear we will not be able to remember the loved one distinctly enough. We want a "piece" of the person we loved, something solid and real to us. One mother told me how she saved a lock of her dead daughter's hair in her jewelry box to look at and to touch. Sometimes a particular piece of clothing, jewelry, art object, book, piece of music, or the like becomes a special object of memory.

Poetry is another meaningful way of giving at the time of a loss. Sharing a poem or a song that we like or that has special meaning to us is a lovely expression of sympathy. Poetry often seems to speak to our deepest recesses and, like music, can have a healing effect. The only sympathy card I remember from twenty years ago, of the hundreds we received, contained a poem I liked that was titled "He's Gone Away." Our identification with, and appreciation of, the metaphor in poetry, fairy tales, and stories encourages us to work through our grief on our deepest levels.

Sharing our spiritual beliefs can also give support to the bereaved, especially if we express uplifting ideas. We can share the solace we have received from our beliefs, but we must never try to push our beliefs on the bereaved. Using another's misfortune to try to "sell" a particular belief system is taking unfair advantage of someone very vulnerable. Each of us must independently choose our own beliefs.

A religious or spiritual person may be a welcome guest for mourners. Loss and death provoke many questions about the meaning of life and death, about why we die, and about afterlife and beyond. A rabbi, minister, priest, or other person with strong spiritual beliefs may help with some of these pressing questions. Some mourners feel so impoverished by their loss that they turn against their former spiritual or religious belief system.

From my own experience, a meaningful and energizing way to be with those in mourning is to meditate with them. If the bereaved are too tense or too self-conscious about meditating themselves, guests might meditate in a separate place, focusing on helping the bereaved to find peace. Meditating, with mourners or separately, means sitting quietly together to relax, to clear the mind, to ease, and to uplift. This can be of great support and is often a relaxing and moving experience for the bereaved and for visitors alike.

For the person who has never meditated before, meditation is simply sitting quietly, eyes closed, intent on relaxing. There are many ways to create this relaxation. One is to watch our breathing or to focus on another sound, apart from ourselves. Quiet music might be played in the background. Another method is to focus on relaxing our whole body part by part. Still another is to count down slowly from fifty to one until we reach a state of relaxation. We can also focus on something apart from ourselves, such as a star or a rainbow or a particular color. Other ways to meditate can be found in the many books on meditation currently available.

Meditation in a group can intensify for each member the state of relaxation. With as few as two or with as many people as are around, the participants simply sit in a circle together, on chairs or on the floor, for ten to twenty minutes of quiet. Meditators might wish to hold hands with each other. If so, the best way to allow free passage of energy among the group members is to hold hands, each person with the right palm turned down and the left palm turned up.

We can sit quietly without any special thought in mind, or we can have a particular focus as a group. It is not necessary for all to have the same focus; we each might have private thoughts or prayers. However, focusing together can be quite moving and powerful. The group can picture whatever it wishes. Or the bereaved can be asked on what the group should focus. The picture might be peace, or recovery for the bereaved, or an easy passing of the soul of the deceased. It can be of great solace to have all one's friends together, focused on healing or on the passage of the soul of a loved one. After the meditation, we may want to share some of our feelings, or something about our reaction to or relationship with the one who died.

Regardless of how we use meditation, the experience of sharing quietly together in this way can be deeply satisfying and consoling for the mourners as well as for the guests. Again, since words often seem so inadequate in offering condolences, meditation is another way—for some a more powerful way—of supporting and sympathizing with grief.

Since the presence of others is such a necessity for the bereaved, it is essential that this needed support not be withdrawn too quickly. It usually takes months after a death for the living to come to terms with the loss. The bereaved need loving support throughout that time. When support is withdrawn suddenly or without warning, it is like another loss. A friend or a group of people might instead take turns checking in periodically with the bereaved in the months following the loss until he or she has recovered. If the person grieving does not seem to be recovering, or seems to be taking an inordinately long time, it is appropriate to suggest that the mourner consult a professional counselor who might be of help.

In summary, there are many ways to assist people in mourning.

It is most important that we do those things that we feel comfortable doing. We should support, not inhibit, the grieving process. The bereaved need to be helped on many levels, be it by our presence, our energy, our sharing, our listening, our weeping together, or the many practical services we have to offer. Even our simplest acts may be of immeasurable value.

10

Helping Ourselves with Grief: Creative Survival

For in the dew of little things the heart
finds its meaning and is refreshed.
                    —The Prophet

To ease our recovery from grief we usually need a great deal of assistance. Often we take for granted our means of support until a crisis comes and we are already in deep need. The three kinds of help that bolster us during grief or any other major crisis in life are self-support, environmental support (the network of people and activities that gives our lives meaning), and the support of our philosophy or belief system. My intent in this chapter is to encourage us to be creative survivors and to expand our supports as insurance for the times when we will be in need. A well-developed support system will enhance the quality of our lives as well.

In a workshop I attended in 1978, Carl and Stephanie Simonton gave the following formula as their idea of an effective support system:

> 25% self-support
> 20% spouse support
> 55% environmental support

This formula offers us a new perspective with which to view our lives. Few of us have so complete a support system. For example, the tendency today is to rely heavily on spouse support, which certainly places a great strain on marriages. This may, in part, be a cause of the high divorce rate. Likewise, our heavy reliance on spouse support may prevent us from personally developing the coping skills we need. When our spouse dies, we may not only suffer an enormous loss of love but also lose most of our support system. Many of us do not involve ourselves socially much beyond our immediate families and our work. We have excuses that we do not have the time or the energy or the need for much else. Thus, we deprive ourselves of much of the extensive environmental support that would benefit us.

Few of us see ourselves as so significant a support as to fulfill 25 percent of our own needs. Therefore, we may fail to attend to expanding our inner resources. In many cases it takes a life crisis, such as a loss or a move, for us to recognize our need for our own love, concern, and support. As important as it is for us to take care of ourselves every day, our need for self-support and self-concern is critical when we are grieving. If we neglect ourselves at such times, we impede our recovery.

Most of all, we need to be able to rely on ourselves in times of trouble. Self-support is a form of self-love. Loving ourselves involves comforting or bolstering ourselves, listening to and accepting our own feelings, paying attention to our physical needs, and making sure that *all* our needs are met rather than ignored.

We need to allow ourselves whatever time it takes us to grieve. Diane Kennedy Pike described taking care of herself through grief as follows:

> I needed to set my own pace for the journey. It might have seemed to someone looking on from the outside that I was walking in place, or even dragging my feet, for I was not ready to turn my attention to the future for many months. But from inside the experience, I was moving as quickly as I could, covering enormous segments of land with a rapidity that used all my energy. Only *I* could know how much time I needed to make each leg of the journey.

We need a lot of encouragement to endure our discomfort and to express ourselves while grieving. We are all tempted at times to run away from tears and uncomfortable feelings like sadness, anger, loneliness, despair, or neediness. As I said before, it takes courage and self-love to believe that experiencing all these feelings will actually help our pain dissolve.

Mourning may require self-supports different from those we are used to. We may need to be more active or more quiet than usual. We may need to talk more or contemplate more. We may need to express feelings out loud or write feelings in a journal. We may need work or responsibility to bolster our self-esteem, or we may need the freedom to take on less responsibility. Most of all, we need to accept our needs, regardless of what we were like before we suffered this loss.

In honoring our feelings and our needs, we can show our concern for ourselves in the simple things we do to make ourselves feel better, like taking hot baths or napping each afternoon. Taking care of ourselves may mean keeping our hands busy or being physically active. Reading during times of stress or trouble may support us. Several people told me that they had read inspirational books after the loss of a loved one. In contrast, one man read books about German concentration camps, for that was the only pain worse to him than his own grief. Some people need to travel to get away from the setting where the loss is most keenly felt. Other people need to take action, to get involved in a cause, perhaps a cause related to the deceased in some way. For example, Art Linkletter, the television personality, became active in an anti-drug campaign after his daughter died during a drug experience. In times of crisis in my own life, I have found great relief in helping others and getting my mind off myself. Our needs in taking care of ourselves are as variable and unique as we are.

Sometimes in order to help us feel better and let go of our grief we need to take some kind of action or create a memorial to the person we loved who is dead. We have very specific and individual needs in this area as well. Simply giving the belongings of the deceased to someone else who is in need may be satisfying enough. Some people have felt a need to dedicate buildings or hospital rooms or books to dead loved ones. For others some kind of memorial fund is a meaningful tribute to the one who is gone. My belief is that our greatest tribute might be in how we live our lives after a loss. Whatever form our tribute takes, it is important that we honor our need for such remembrance.

Our belief system is another important means of support. Whether our beliefs actually sustain us through a crisis is, of course, an individual matter. Our philosophy of life, however, very much affects how well we cope with pain and problems. The meanings we ascribe to life, to suffering, and to death are often the keys to how well we survive the pain and how we restructure our lives after a loss. Living a life of meaning, whatever meaning that may be, is easier than living without spiritual values. For example, people who can accept sorrow and crises as part of their own growth and development find that their beliefs are deeply supportive in their healing and recovery.

In years gone by, finding effective supports outside ourselves was less of a problem. We lived amid extended families where we were often surrounded by others who could be immediately available to help us with whatever problems arose. Now we live in isolated units, as individuals, small family groups, and frequently in one-parent families, where other adults with whom to share the stresses of life are missing. Without the immediacy of family supports, we are forced to create our own support systems. Unfortunately, many of us do not take responsibility for this kind of expansion. Hence, we have very inadequate supports in our lives and find ourselves often in desperate need when trouble arrives.

How people get the support they need to survive crisis or trauma has always been fascinating to me. So often people have told me the answer was their *friends.* A dramatic example of this was my friend Tom, mentioned earlier, who upon learning that he might have terminal cancer called old friends all over the country and shared his feelings with them. What he created was a countrywide network of support, consisting of phone calls, letters, and visits that have enriched his life and encouraged him to go on. Close friends can make the critical difference in our coping with grief.

A wide range of people and activities comprise our environmental support system. Here are some of these supports:

ENVIRONMENTAL SUPPORTS

People	*Other*
Intimates	Adult community college courses
Family	Job or job change or guidance
Friends	Volunteer work
Neighbors	Women's/men's clubs
Colleagues	Pet
Family physician	Travel
Health care professionals	Move
Psychotherapist/counselor	Remarriage
Clergy	Art
Lawyer	Music
Insurance agent	Dance
Financial adviser	Bereavement groups
Funeral director	Other self-help groups
Local businesspeople	Sports
	Meditation

The more people and activities we have in our lives, the more expanded and useful our support system. Examining all the aspects of our support system is a way for each of us to be more conscious of the means for creating more satisfying lives for ourselves and, therefore, to be more in control. Developing a full support system enhances our creative survival.

While we are grieving, we may not feel very resourceful, so in order to be a creative survivor we may need to recall how we coped in the past, what our needs were and what helped us. Where did we get the most support? Meditation? Suspension of regular routines? Involvement in activities? Work? Leisure? Home? Travel away from home? Our awareness of how we handled difficult times in the past can help us cope with our present problems.

All of us could probably benefit from enlarging our current support systems. It might be a good idea to make a list of all the people and activities we would add to our lives right now if we could. Include activities, hobbies, courses, or skills we always wanted to explore further. Each of us has phantom interests, dream hobbies, or careers we never pursued. We might think, too, of people we wish we knew better or people we have lost touch with or do not see as often as we wish. The list of environmental supports can be used as a guideline.

Another way of exploring possible activities for ourselves is one I learned from a ten-year-old friend, Laurie Snyder, who used to have a list on her bedroom door, THINGS LAURIE CAN DO WHEN SHE'S ALONE. On this list Laurie had written twenty or thirty activities to occupy herself when she imagined she had nothing to do. Often after a loss we have difficulty in resuming life, especially if we are alone for the first time. Such a list has been a useful tool for myself and my clients. Writing down the possibilities open to us is a way to reach our untapped resources. Here is a sample:

THINGS I CAN DO WHEN I AM ALONE

Listen to music
Write music
Read novels, mysteries, health books, magazines, etc.
Write letters
Write short stories
Draw or paint
Take photographs
Make jewelry
Sew, knit, crochet, or needlepoint
Make a scrapbook, photo album
Collect stamps or coins, etc.
Play solitaire
Work crossword puzzles
Work jigsaw puzzles
Learn a new subject
Learn how to do my own income taxes
Build
Refinish furniture
Redecorate

Frame pictures	Walk, hike, or run
Plan a trip	Clean a closet
Garden	Go to a movie, concert, play
Gather wood for fireplace	Shop

After we have drawn up a list of relationships and activities we would like to pursue, we need to be willing to follow up on these new ideas. Depending on our responsibilities, we might decide to seek out at least one new person or pursue one new activity each week, or one each month. We might plan our moves ahead of time on a calendar. In this program to expand our lives, we should try to follow up on at least one of these items immediately to support our persevering with our new goals. Knowing how temporary life is, we should take heed and do whatever we intend to do, right now.

Sometimes group support enhances our willingness to follow through with new ideas. We can join already-existing groups, or we might bring a group of friends or colleagues together to experiment with one of our ideas. For example, a woman who wanted to exercise regularly found a teacher and a place, and she scheduled twice-weekly classes for all the neighborhood women, ten to twenty of whom came regularly and shared the costs and the experience. Taking initiative for creating a new activity may encourage others to join, and they in turn might initiate another activity that would include us. For example, several years ago I created a women's consciousness-raising group with seven acquaintances. At the end of six weeks we were so fond of each other that we decided to continue meeting weekly to pursue our metaphysical interests. We taught each other to meditate and shared many new ideas together. Not only did we continue to stimulate one another's growth, we also were an important support in each other's lives. We became a sort of extended family to rely on in all times of need.

Groups are rewarding, for they offer an opportunity to get back more than we put in. But like any relationships, groups need nurturing in order to survive. Many of us take our relationships for granted, fail to put our full energy into them, and then find they are not there when we need them. Often we confuse our priorities and needs and do not fulfill our important needs for contact, intimacy, and sharing. We make excuses for not expanding our lives; we say that it takes too much time. Of course, it does take time and energy to expand our relationships, but invariably it is worth the effort.

Death education can be a great support. Nowadays more and more communities and colleges are offering courses on understanding and exploring death and dying. There are many books on this subject, several of which are listed in the bibliography at the back of this book. (See also chapter 15.)

A bereavement group is also valuable while grieving. There is one in my community, sponsored by the adult education department of a high school, which meets two to three hours a week. Anyone is welcome to attend for as long as needed. At one time the group included eight women, ages twenty-six to ninety, all of whom were dealing with dying or dead husbands. They supported each other emotionally through several deaths, and they were of practical help to one another as well. One dying man with several children had no will, and his worried wife felt they could not afford legal help. Another group member arranged for her lawyer brother to donate time to help all members of the bereavement group write wills. On another occasion a dying man came to the group to find out what his wife was doing there. He ended up talking at length for the first time about his own impending death. Strangers can often give so much to each other.

There are other kinds of groups to help the bereaved. For example, in San Francisco there is a group called the Shanti Project, which trains people to act as counselors for the dying and their families. Another group that meets in many cities is the Widowed Persons Service Program. Widows and widowers from this group reach out to the bereaved, often through reading death notices in the newspapers. The sharing of a fellow sufferer who has survived sorrow is one of the greatest supports for the grieving.

Meditation can be another form of help—both for every day and for times of crisis. Techniques for meditation were discussed in chapter 9 and can also be learned through books or teachers. Meditating can be uplifting, healing, and tension-releasing. Not only does meditating calm us, it may also enable us to gain a larger perspective on issues in our lives. This can be of particular help when grieving.

An invaluable support when grieving is psychotherapy, which is the unique experience of relating to a caring, supportive person who does not need us and who is detached enough to allow us to grieve fully without interference. The psychotherapist, whether a social worker, psychologist, psychiatrist, or counselor, can help us express ourselves, understand ourselves, examine our options, re-create our goals, gain new perspective, complete our grief, and restore our lives.

For most of us, choosing appropriate help for ourselves is difficult. It is even harder when we are in the midst of suffering. Therefore, we need to recognize that communication and rapport, as well as real help with the crisis of our grief, are what make for successful psychotherapy. The "right" therapist is one whom we experience as understanding, helpful, and knowledgeable about grief.

If we do not know a psychotherapist to call, we can get recommendations from friends, physicians, lawyers, clergy, social agencies, or the psychiatric departments of local hospitals. But no matter who refers us for therapy, we must feel free to make the ultimate decision as to whether or not this feels like the person who can help us.

Because psychotherapy outside a clinic situation can be expensive, we may not be willing to pay for interviews with a variety of counselors to find the one who feels best. So initially we may use the telephone in searching for help. If finding a therapist seems an overwhelming task for a grieving individual, a friend or relative might do some initial calling of therapists to find the appropriate person. However, many psychotherapists require that the actual arranging of the first appointment be done only by the prospective client as a statement of the client's genuine interest in the therapy.

Before examining the specifics of selecting a psychotherapist, it is important to note that a major pitfall in choosing a therapist is the tendency to assume that a professional is an expert because of his or her title. Not all psychotherapists and counselors are effective in assisting with grief. Therefore, as prospective clients we are responsible for finding ourselves a sensitive, wise counselor. Many of us are apt to give so much power or weight to the professional that we immediately blame ourselves for any lack of rapport or success in therapy, rather than seeing any problems or imperfections in the "expert."

Following are some guidelines for selecting a psychotherapist. First, we need to find the best counselor for our circumstances. Mainly we want to avoid a psychotherapist who is not at ease confronting grief. It is also important that the therapist view grief not as a disease but as a natural and necessary process that precedes healing. We want a therapist willing to focus on *now*, on our current feelings, rather than primarily on the past, which might serve to avoid our grief. We may also want the counselor to have expertise specifically in resolving grief.

Second, we need to tell the prospective counselor our problems as well as our aims in therapy. For example, "My husband died three months ago and I have felt immobilized ever since" or "I have symptoms of tiredness and shortness of breath since my mother's death six months ago" or "I need to talk out my feelings about my father's death with someone outside my family" or "I have been unable to finish grieving on my own and want professional help."

Third, after saying what we want, we may have some questions for the professional. For example, "Is grief an area of your expertise, or would you recommend someone else who does work well with grief? What kind of therapy do you do? Will you focus with me on my present problem, or do you emphasize history and the past? Will you see me on a short-term basis, or do you only take clients for a long-term commitment to therapy?" It is valid to select a therapist who knows about grief, who is willing to work on a short-term basis or in an as-needed contract with clients, and who focuses on the present.

Fourth, we need to look at the issue of taking psychiatric medications such as tranquilizers and antidepressants, which can be prescribed only by a psychiatrist or other physician. Medication may be necessary to help a grieving person sleep. Drugs may also be appropriate in the initial phase of grief, when we are in shock. But medication will not help us cope directly with grief or resolve it once we are ready to face our feelings. If a psychotherapist offers only medication to a grieving client, the therapist is avoiding facing the emotional aspects of grief and a change of therapists is probably in order. The temptation to avoid and cover our pain always exists. Drugs are one way we can purposely numb ourselves. Although external substances may offer temporary relief from our suffering, such help is not the ultimate solution for resolving our grief.

Fifth, we need to know the kind of therapy available to us. Up to now the emphasis has been on individual counseling. Although this is often more expensive, it is an opportunity for us to be the sole focus of attention. In group therapy we share time with others and gain the stimulation and support of others' ideas and experiences. Weekend workshops offer an intensity of experience that can be deep, meaningful, and provocative. Family therapy focuses on the family as a functioning unit, which may be useful for a grieving family. It is of great value for a client to experience more than one psychotherapist, for each may have his or her own brand of wisdom or experience to share.

In summary, how we help ourselves through grief very much depends on our self-support, our environmental support, and our belief system. In order to be a creative survivor, it is essential that we fully develop all the supports available to us, both to enhance the quality of our lives and as insurance for future times when we may be in great need.

11

Recovery from Grief

. . . That your passion may live through
its own daily resurrection, and like
the phoenix rise above its own ashes.
—The Prophet

Although it may be hard to believe, we can recover from our
sorrow. Recovery from grief is the restoration of our capacity
for living a full life and enjoying life without feelings of guilt,
shame, sorrow, or regret. We have recovered when we once again
feel able to cope with our feelings and our environment, and
when we can face reality and accept our loss on a gut level,
not just intellectually. Integrating our loss and reinvesting in our
lives constitute recovery.

The process of recovering from grief is very much like the
old song about love to the effect that the song is over but the
melody lingers. The depth of sorrow, the pain, the weeping, the
incapacitation, the neediness, and all the intense feelings of
mourning eventually diminish and disappear. We do not forget
the loved one or the loss, but the pain recedes. Usually the dissolv-
ing of grief is gradual rather than sudden. In the process of recovering, grief may be triggered unexpectedly many times before
completion. We may go through different waves of pain, until
the waves stop coming. Once we recover, the gap left by the
loss may still be evident, but our reactions to it will be less intense.

Recovery results from setting recovery as an essential goal and
from living each day as it comes, dealing with both the regular
routine of living and our deepest emotions. We are recovering
when we can look at life ahead as worth living. Full recovery

involves having the perspective to realize that someday we will look back and know that we have fully grieved and survived life's darkest hours.

Whether we experience it or not, grief accompanies all the major changes in our lives. When we realize that we have grieved before and recovered, we see that we may recover this time as well. It is more natural to recover and go on living than to halt in the tracks of grief forever. In his book *Choices,* Frederic Flach says, "Most people who become depressed recover. Most creative, accomplished people have reported periods of depression just before a new surge of personal growth and achievement."

The low self-esteem that is characteristic of the mourning period often interferes with our believing that we can recover from grief. The experience of loss temporarily destroys our self-confidence, and the process of grieving depletes much of our energy. As we begin to recover, our energy increases and our self-esteem usually returns. But hanging on to such feelings as guilt or shame or resentment will delay the return of our self-confidence.

Our expectations, willingness, and beliefs are all essential to our recovery from grief. It is right to *expect* to recover, no matter how great the loss. Recovery is the normal way. When we expect to recover, and know it is possible, we set recovery as a goal to reach for. On the other hand, if we get caught up in the popular belief that the pain of loss is never-ending, we doom ourselves to feelings of hopelessness and continued sorrow.

Willingness to recover is essential. What it takes to recover is a willingness to hope, a willingness to go on with one's life, a willingness to let go of the pain, and a willingness to heal fully. If we cannot find such willingness inside ourselves, we need to examine our resistances to healing.

As mentioned earlier, there are cultural barriers to recovery from which some of our resistances stem. One popular misconception is that to grieve a long time is a sign of our love for the deceased. The converse, then, is that if we recover quickly from grief, we did not truly love. Another false idea is that mourners should look "bad," either physically or in terms of their coping in the world. A healthy, robust-looking mourner, or a mourner who is functioning reasonably well again, is sometimes distrusted or misjudged by the less aware outsider. Perhaps the most destructive misconception about grief is that if we loved the deceased we would not go on living our lives. These are poisonous ideas for the mourner.

The truth is that after a major loss it is healthiest to take care of ourselves and to reconstruct our lives. On all levels life is a process of continual renewal. Spring does not refuse to come because it was preceded by winter.

Negative beliefs are the other major barrier to recovery. To recover, we need to believe that full recovery of ourselves and our lives is possible. Beliefs often become self-fulfilling prophecies, which means that we act according to the way we believe, creating our own reality. In other words, if we have seen one person who never recovered after a loss, we may then generalize that experience and create a belief that people do not recover from the loss of a loved one. Thus, recovery seems an impossibility. When we give in to such false ideas, we doom ourselves to endless grief.

Similarly, after a loss we may hang on to a certain feeling, such as guilt or resentment or disappointment, that immobilizes us. Often people do not believe that a feeling will ever go away, and that is how they keep the feeling alive. We may hang on to certain fears, such as a fear of the future, and thus keep ourselves stuck in the past. This is why it is crucial that we examine our beliefs and attitudes about recovery in order for our mental health and life to be restored after the death of a loved one.

Again, recovery from grief is normal. Therefore, if we believe in recovery, we can set in motion a positive self-fulfilling prophecy. "I will recover" can become a beacon of light on the difficult road of grieving.

The process of restoring or renewing ourselves calls on all our personal strengths and resources. It is not easy, but it is worth-

while. We may have to be flexible as well as willing to change
some of our attitudes and values. A loss may force us to re-
evaluate our lives as well as make some changes.

Let us look at an example of the kind of attitude change we
might need to make in order to re-create our lives after a loss.
Imagine believing that life can be pleasurable only if one is married, and then losing your mate. You now have a choice: you
can give up on life, because according to your belief system life
can no longer offer you pleasure, or you can change. What you
believe will affect what happens next. Many of us hold beliefs,
such as this one, that inhibit us from moving ahead with our
lives. In order to live, we must alter our ideas about life.

How can we change a belief? We begin the process of change
by becoming aware that beliefs affect the outcome of our lives.
Beliefs are like habits that we get used to, take for granted, and
never re-examine. Next we notice *what* we believe. To do that
we might sit down and write out every belief we can think of
in regard to recovering from grief. If we are not sure what we
believe, we can write down everything we have ever heard on
the subject of grieving.

After we have made our list, we need to put it aside for several
days and then reread it. In this way we can examine each belief
individually and ask ourselves some questions. For example, Is
this truly my belief, or is it something someone else has taught
me? Does this habit or belief make sense to me now? Does this
belief fit into my life? Do I want to keep this belief? If we take
a good look at our responses to these questions, we can see
whether our beliefs are still positive, supportive, and fitting for
us. Simply examining our beliefs in this way is a start toward
changing them.

Here are some other exercises we might try in order to alter
our beliefs. First, we can talk about our attitudes with a friend.
What is his or her reaction? What are his or her own beliefs in
this area? Second, we can gather beliefs from a variety of people
on the same subject. We might write them down so that we

can examine them all at once. And then we should re-examine our own beliefs.

Another technique is to find someone we know who does not believe as we do and discuss our beliefs together. For example, if we believe that marriage is the only happy state possible for a woman, we should talk with a satisfied single woman and listen to her contrasting point of view. If we believe that recovery from grief is impossible, we can look for someone who has fully recovered from grief and ask that person about his or her experience with grief and recovery. With all these techniques, we can challenge our old belief systems, just as the loss itself has challenged us to rethink our lives.

In some cases it may be necessary to work hard at examining the beliefs that might be getting in our way. But in the process of personal restoration, shifts in beliefs and behavior may occur naturally. For example, I knew a shy man who seemed to blossom socially after his wife died. He became talkative, charming, and more aware of world issues. He told me his wife had always done the talking, and sometimes the thinking, for both of them. He felt he had to fill the gap her death left in his life by doing for himself what his wife had done for him.

Another example of a natural shift occurred in a woman named Jan, married to a pianist, a creative, exciting man, who died unexpectedly. She was devastated by the loss. As she grieved, she imagined she would never again know such an extraordinary man. That turned out to be true. When Jan remarried a few years later, her new husband was not like the pianist in any way. Through the process of grieving, she had discovered that she wanted a different kind of marriage. She did not want to be the audience and support for another self-centered artist, no matter how extraordinary he might be.

In addition to our expectations, willingness, and beliefs about recovery, there are some personal attributes that help us restore ourselves more quickly and easily after an emotional crisis. *Courage* is a great asset for facing any difficulty in life. The courage to grieve, to experience and face our feelings, and the courage to go on with life, all are potent tools for restoring ourselves. *Patience* with ourselves and with the natural process of grieving is another great help in recovery. Being able to bear and tolerate our pain and misfortune propels us into resolution and growth. *Resilience,* the capacity to bounce back from stress and go on, is a valuable tool. It is a popular belief that as we get older we have limited emotional resilience because we are less resilient physically. The opposite is more likely. Emotional resilience is learned and tends to increase rather than decrease as we age. The more suffering we experience in our lives, the more we learn how to incorporate our pain and cope with suffering. *Perseverance* or *endurance,* having the faith that staying with whatever we are experiencing will get us through it, is another valuable strength. A *capacity to distance,* the ability to step back and view life from afar, is one of the greatest assets for all kinds of personal problem-solving. It is important to be able to move out of the intensity of feelings, or at times out of the drama of our lives, to gain perspective in order to cope and to move ahead. A *sense of humor,* whatever your personal brand of humor may be, is a great help to recovery. It is a relief to be able to laugh at life sometimes, to take pain less seriously, even if only for a moment.

Some of us may berate ourselves for lacking some or all of these stellar qualities. Yet each of us has the potential to develop all these assets and more. It is as if we keep these qualities dormant in ourselves. We must allow our abilities for coping to develop, and in this way we can re-create our own resources. Often we have strengths and abilities that we never really put to the test. Now is the time for us to discover these assets in ourselves and draw them out, to look for personal resources we may not have imagined existed before. It is our beliefs and our old pictures of ourselves that can most prevent us from developing our full potential.

Here are some techniques that can give us the opportunity to experiment with some of the qualities that assist in recovery from grief and in growth of any kind. We should put aside some time to be quiet and relaxed and practice these techniques. If the suggestions are hard for us to follow at first, we should remain patient. New learning can sometimes be awkward, but the resources we can gain are worth repeated effort.

First, we need to take time to imagine ourselves as having each of the individual assets that I have just mentioned. It is a mistake for us to get involved with the qualities we *think* we might have. Instead, we should allow ourselves to assume that we are first courageous, then patient, and so on. If the quality feels unfamiliar now, we can picture a time in the past when we were, for example, courageous. Do we ever remember in our lives an experience where we knew we possessed courage? Virtually everyone can. Once that memory is implanted, we should examine the experience in detail. If we like, we can repeat the procedure, picturing other times when we showed courage. What we are doing is making real for ourselves that forgotten asset. We should review each of these assets in this way, and if we choose we can add to the list other assets that might be valuable. If we have any trouble picturing ourselves with one or more of these qualities, it is a simple matter to picture someone else who is patient, courageous, resilient, or whatever. Then we can imagine we are like that person. Again, we should deal with each of these qualities, one at a time.

Another technique for working with personal qualities that seem to be missing in ourselves is to *affirm* that we have whatever the missing trait may be. An affirmation is a statement or assertion of truth or fact. Affirmations, therefore, can become self-fulfilling prophecies. Of course, our affirmations should always be positive rather than negative statements.

The most important rule for making an affirmation is that you *desire* whatever it is you affirm. In addition to wanting what you affirm, picture it and say it. The technique for affirming goes as follows. First, we write down a positive statement in the present tense that asserts a quality we would like to possess. Each sentence should be a "now" sentence rather than something in the future tense. For example, "I am courageous," not "I will be courageous." By using the present tense, we put whatever we are affirming within our reach. Other examples of affirmations might be "I am strong," "I am resilient," or "I can cope well with my life."

So that our affirmation will fit our particular situation more precisely, we can change the affirmation accordingly. Specific personal details should be included. For example, "I have the strength to face my grief and finish with it" or "I have the courage to live alone now that my spouse is gone."

We can say our affirmations out loud to ourselves several times a day. Another effective technique is to write or type the positive statement ten to fifteen times, once or twice each day. Affirmations help us focus our energies on the actions we wish to have occur in our lives.

Sometimes we may find ourselves resisting or unwilling to believe the affirmation we have chosen. Hence, it is worthwhile to write down our reaction to the affirmation. For example, we can divide a page in half and on the left side write our affirmation and on the right side write our reactions to it. Here is an example of this method for using affirmations as an opportunity to disclose our deeper feelings:

Affirmation	*Reaction*
I, Judy, am courageous.	I am not. I'm scared.
I, Judy, am courageous.	I am not now. I wish I were.
I, Judy, am courageous.	I feel scared now. But I remember when I decided to get through my freshman year of college, even though I was more scared than I am right now.
I, Judy, am courageous.	It sounds so good. I wish I were.

If we wish to make several affirmations, it is best to focus on one at a sitting. However, we can do two in a day at different times, or alternate one the first day, another the second, then back to the first one on the third day, and so forth. A rule of thumb is to keep making the chosen affirmation for as long a period as it takes for the change affirmed to occur, whether that be days or months. The more we believe in what we are doing, the more quickly affirmations become truth. Some affirmations become fact immediately, simply because we acknowledge the truth in ourselves.

One woman who was having difficulty recovering from the end of a relationship decided to experiment with affirmations. Because she was unwilling to socialize or reach out into the world to help herself recover from her grief, she was more attracted to staying at home and making affirmations for a couple of hours every day. She said the process felt meditative and quieting for her as she wrote again and again all the changes she wanted to occur in her life. Within a few weeks, she noticed that she was feeling buoyant and free of depression. Soon she met a new friend and began considering a return to work. After a month of making affirmations, she called to tell me she felt fully recovered.

Affirmations are found in many different systems for personal growth. A currently popular book on affirmations is Sondra Ray's *I Deserve Love.*

Setting future goals is also important for recovery from grief. By setting goals we affirm life and help give structure to the road ahead. It is always worthwhile to stop for a moment and ask ourselves, What do I want right now in my life? In their book *Getting Well Again,* the Simontons offer many suggestions for useful goal-setting. They recommend that goals be concrete, specific, measurable, and realistic. The setting of goals has many purposes, some of which are to help us reinvest in life, to reinforce our wish to go on, to take more responsibility for our lives, to build self-confidence, and to help us focus our energies.

It is valuable during recovery from grief for us to set both long-term goals and short-term ones. Short-term goals, those within one or two weeks, might be as simple as "I will go to a movie" or "I will get my hair done this week." Or they may be more complex, such as "I will go out on at least one job interview" or "I will repaint my kitchen." Goals of one month might be to dispose of the belongings of the deceased, to finish one's correspondence, to begin an exercise class, to plan a trip, or even to have a job. Goals set further in the future might relate to work, vacations, pleasurable activities, moving, health care, or whatever wants or needs one wishes to have met. Affirmations can help in this goal-setting process.

Another technique that helps in setting goals is one I call "The I-Want Exercise." As homework in therapy, I encourage clients to practice thinking, saying aloud, and writing "I want" as often as possible. Because we feel low or unworthy, we are apt to shut off wanting. Allowing ourselves to want something is revitalizing and helps us find a new sense of direction. At first people may notice that their wants are very simple, like "I want a drink of water" or "I want to read my newspaper now." But the more attention we pay to ourselves, the more we are likely to discover our deeper, more heartfelt wants, like "I want more love in my life" or "I want to feel closer to my children" or "I want to explore ideas for changing my career."

As we recover from grief, some of us grow and develop new strengths naturally. Usually we need some support as well as new ideas to speed our recovery and growth. That is why this is an opportune time to seek the help of a professional, such as a psychologist, social worker, psychiatrist, family counselor, minister, or some kind of recovery or self-help group. Often the professional can help us examine our beliefs and deficiencies, as well as support us in considering options to take that will bring about the changes we desire in our lives. How to seek professional help was discussed in detail in chapter 10.

Facing a loss in our life can force a major revision in our sense of ourselves. We can and should take an active part in that revision. Such changes may be essential for us to restore our lives and continue living. Recovery, then, means being open to more change.

For total recovery from a loss, we must finish, or complete, our grief. That is the subject of the next chapter.

PART FOUR

Grief Resolution

12
Finishing

Your pain is the breaking of the shell
that encloses your understanding.
          —The Prophet

Ideally, when we love someone who has died, we must thoroughly
experience all the feelings evoked by our loss and then say good-
bye to our loved one and resume our lives. To recover fully from
a loss means to finish or completely let go. Finishing with a dead
loved one does not erase the love or the memories, but it does
mean that we have accepted the death, that the pain and sorrow
have lessened, and that we feel free to reinvest in our lives.

The concept of finishing comes from Gestalt therapy, which
holds that we can finish or complete any experience in life, that
what is past can truly be relinquished. Finishing involves directly
experiencing or expressing anew or again all the emotions connected with the unfinished situation, experiencing the full impact
again in the now, until all the feelings are dissipated. The goal
of finishing is to move feelings or experiences from foreground
to background, to gain relief, and to attain some shift in perspective.

If we do not finish with our grief, we experience the problems
and symptoms of unsuccessful grief mentioned in chapter 7. What
is unfinished in the grief process usually relates to sorrow, anger,
unfulfilled wishes, and any other unexpressed feelings. Often
we are unwilling to let go and to let our loved one be dead. In
order to cope with the intensity of grief, we may deny some or
all of our feelings, mistakenly believing that our grief will then
be easier. Sometimes we suppress feelings that seem unacceptable

to us. Unfortunately, denying grief causes our pain, distress, and inability to let go of the deceased to persist. Unfinished situations are filled with the same emotion and intensity as ever, even years later.

Sometimes our grief is unfinished because the means we used to complete our grief are not effective. For example, ruminating about and being obsessed with sorrow are necessary in the first flush of mourning, but they are ineffective completion tools months after death occurs. Attempts to rationalize or think ourselves out of grief are circular. We run around the same track again and again without the necessary break in perspective that emotional release provokes in completing a grief experience. Trying to reason ourselves out of grief, or out of any feeling, rarely works. Likewise, swallowing feelings, or pretending that feelings are gone, are ways in which we fool ourselves into thinking we are finished with grief. Disowned or denied feelings do not simply disappear.

Often our grief is unfinished because we have found no comfortable means to release the complicated and mixed feelings we may have had about the deceased or the former relationship. In long relationships, we typically build up a great deal of unfinished business for which we have no means of dissipation. In our society it is unusual for people to be fully open and truthful in intimate relationships. As a result, we more than likely have much that is unspoken and therefore unfinished, and it is these things that may plague us when our loved ones die. We need a *direct* way of finishing, which the Gestalt therapy approach offers.

There are various indications of unfinished grief, which were discussed in detail in chapter 7. The most obvious is when one is still in mourning years after the event. We know we are unfinished when we are preoccupied with the deceased, or more involved with the deceased than with our own lives. Other symptoms that may indicate unfinished grief are anxiety, fearfulness (especially fear of death), depression, deadening of emotions, suicidal thoughts, sleep difficulties, and physical symptoms that have no obvious organic cause. Sometimes problems in our relationships indicate our unfinished grief, such as difficulty in forming new relationships, reluctance to trust or be close, lack of interest in others, or excessive need for other people. Difficulty in proceeding with life, long after a loss, is another major sign of probable unfinished grief.

Learning how to finish is an important skill for each of us to develop, whether we are facing finishing with dead people or with live ones, finishing with old experiences or old aspects of ourselves. How long it will take to finish grieving is an individual matter. Living with and expressing grief feelings is healthy and necessary in the first months after a loss. Depending on how important the lost loved one was to the survivor, healthy finishing can occur as early as three months after the loss or as long as a year or two later. Whenever unfinished feelings are perceived, even years later, it is time to finish. It is never too late to complete our grief.

The Gestalt therapy technique for finishing involves facing our problems directly. We do this by imagining that we are placing the person or the problem with which we are struggling in a chair facing us. We then carry on a dialogue aloud with that person, or problem, until we reach some kind of resolution. If this is a new approach, it may seem awkward at first, as new learning can be. Therefore, we need to see what we are doing as an experiment rather than a performance or a test. Talking aloud promotes honesty with ourselves and enables us to hear our inner feelings. We may wish to carry on this dialogue alone, or we may want to have a friend or loved one with us. I prefer the support of a listener. The format that follows can be used as is, or it can be elaborated upon or altered to fit our particular circumstances.

TECHNIQUE FOR FINISHING

First, ask yourself, Do I want to finish? If the answer is yes, sit down facing an empty chair. Remain seated quietly for a few minutes, and breathe deeply to help yourself relax. Now imagine that the person (or object, experience, memory, or whatever) with whom you wish to finish is seated in the chair opposite you. Imagine focusing your thoughts and feelings on the person or issue at hand. Then begin by sharing *out loud* whatever comes to mind, any feeling that this experience evokes. It is essential that you be true to yourself, which means that you allow yourself to express whatever you feel. Sentences that begin with "I" best elicit feelings. One way to begin might be to express your discomfort about doing this kind of dialogue, or to express feelings such as "I have never been able to say good-bye to you" or "I have carried around my sorrow at losing you for years now" or "I still feel angry at you" or "I have never had any feelings or reactions to your death."

Your feelings may rush forth after your opening sentence. That is the time to say whatever you feel, aloud. If you do not feel much happening for you, or if you feel stuck, you can try saying either "I am angry at you" or "I am still angry at you for dying," or the reverse, "I am sad" or "I still miss you." Usually then your true feelings will come to the surface.

These simple, straightforward, and emotionally charged expressions are designed to enable you to evoke your own deeper feelings. It is best to take time to check out what feels true for you. Whatever feeling emerges naturally is a true one. If you experiment with a feeling that does not seem to fit or something that feels false, drop that expression or feeling. If you suspect you have more feelings in one area than are emerging, stay with those and keep repeating a sentence that represents the feelings, like "I am sad," until the feelings begin to rise within you. Bottled-up feelings need to be encouraged to come out into the open. If you have trouble knowing what feelings you have suppressed, you can review chapter 3, "The Mourning Period," where many different feelings are described.

You may feel certain that you have no anger, for example, at the deceased. Nevertheless, check out your feelings by saying aloud several times "I am angry at you . . ." to discover what the truth is. You might also try the reverse, "I am not angry at you," to see if that feels true.

When we finally admit our formerly suppressed anger, sometimes expressing it aloud in a dialogue does not feel satisfying enough. I have several tools to help my clients fully express their anger. First of all, the louder the anger is expressed, the more satisfying it is. Also, pounding, kicking, jumping on, or squeezing a pillow assists some in fully releasing anger. I also use an old tennis racket, held in both hands, to hit a pillow or mattress again and again in the process of expressing anger or rage. Throwing dishes, hitting a punching bag, yelling in a closet or the shower, slamming doors, tearing up old books, and running are some of the means my clients use to release their anger fully.

Often a central part of the process of finishing is acknowledging that the person is truly gone. If one is denying the death, it is necessary to confront such truths as "I know you are dead" or "I know I am not going to see you again." Admitting the death can be a great relief.

Understanding and finishing with loss hinges on our admitting *what* we lost. Knowing precisely what is now gone enables us to grieve fully and perhaps fill that gap in the future. Here are some examples, to help us identify for ourselves what is unique in our own loss.

She was my best friend, my favorite person to talk with.
He was always there for me no matter what, and without him
  I feel all alone.
She was the first person who seemed to understand me.
He accepted me completely with all my faults.
She was the most loving person I ever knew.
He would literally give me the shirt off his back.
She made me laugh like no one I ever knew.
He always gave me such good advice.

Another key expression that may evoke hidden feelings about a loss is "I wish . . ." It is helpful to begin one or several sentences with "I wish" and see what emerges. Often our secret wishes keep us from letting go or from coping with the loss in a more constructive, life-affirming way.

During a dialogue that is geared toward finishing, we may notice body sensations or reactions that are unusual to us, such as tears, shaking, dizziness, excessive heat or cold, or the like. These are natural reactions. Your body is reacting along with your emotions to the intensity of feelings that were formerly suppressed or denied. There is no need to fear these body sensations, which are simply confirming your emotional state. They will disappear after your emotions are expressed and released.

In addition to or instead of the kind of dialogue just mentioned, you may want to express *aloud* your appreciations and resentments to the person you are imagining sitting opposite you. For example, you might begin by listing aloud everything you appreciated about the deceased. When you feel you are through, you may pause and then list all your resentments, or vice versa. In this way you can see what feelings you may have held back, what you learn about yourself, and what you learn about the relationship. Expressing appreciations and resentments can be very helpful in enabling us to let go.

Whatever feelings you are expressing, continue your dialogue until you feel you have no more to say. If you are unsure whether there is more, you can try saying aloud, "I feel finished with you now." Then you can try the reverse, "I don't feel finished with you yet." Either of these might be true for you. If you are still not sure, you can keep repeating these contrasting ideas until one or the other feels true. Similarly, you might use the sentence "I am ready to say good-bye to you now," or "I am not ready to say good-bye to you yet." When you feel ready, you can say good-bye, and whatever saying good-bye entails for you, being sure to express fully the feelings that emerge in and around saying good-bye.

Carrying on such a dialogue is a profound tool for tapping inner feelings and moving toward resolution of guilt or other problems. In addition, you may want to play the role of the deceased person with whom you have been speaking. Although you may feel awkward or skeptical about being the other person, playing the role of the other can be an opportunity for objectivity and real insight. To change roles, sit where you imagined the deceased to be sitting earlier, and face the seat where you were sitting. Then allow yourself to respond or to speak for the deceased. If it feels right, this dialogue can be continued *between* you and the deceased, changing chairs as you do so. Each person in the dialogue then has a chance for self-expression and completion. Even though you create this dialogue, it can have a great impact and will allow you to examine your contrasting feelings. Although you may feel self-conscious or skeptical, risking this kind of experience may enable you to finish grieving.

The technique of carrying on a dialogue directly with a photograph of the dead person can intensify the reality of the experience. Likewise, dialogues surrounded by some of the belongings of the deceased can help you tap your deepest feelings, perhaps more easily than without such aids. These devices may be painfully difficult to use in the early stages of grief, and easier later on. Much of the finishing work I have done with clients has been without the benefit of photographs or other memorabilia of the deceased and yet was profoundly effective.

Another method for dialogue with a dead person is to first close your eyes and picture the person. Then, aloud, call to that person by name. You can keep calling until your grief feelings emerge. The dialogue can then be continued in any of the ways mentioned earlier.

EXAMPLES OF FINISHINGS

It was out of my personal experience with Gestalt therapy that I finally completed my grief with my brother, fourteen long years after his death, in a professional training workshop with James S. Simkin, an outstanding Gestalt therapist. That experience was so moving that I would like to share it here in detail.

From a recurrent angry dream I hoped to work on in the group, Jim asked me who was I angry at then. I said, without much feeling, "I guess I was angry at my parents and angry at my brother dying." Immediately, Jim put an empty chair in front of me and said, "Tell your brother that you are angry at him for dying." I gasped. What a confrontation! I wanted to run away and hide.

Although I had cried and cried over David's death, never before had I acknowledged in any way that I might have been angry at "poor David" for dying. I felt very shaken.

I began, unsurely, "David, I am angry at you for dying." Suddenly a flood of feelings emerged. Mainly, I felt angry that David had died before teaching me the things about boys and dating that, as an older brother, he had promised to teach me. I felt angry that he had left me when I was feeling so vulnerable, that he had left me feeling so responsible for being the only child now with my parents, that he had left me lonely, and that he was gone and would never come back to be with me again. Up to that moment, anger at David seemed wrong, inappropriate, selfish, or unfair. Now I cried with pain and relief. My sorrow had been well expressed many times before; it was my anger that seemed totally new.

Jim paused and then said, "Now say good-bye to David." I know I must have looked at Jim with horror. Good-bye seemed a terrible word. However, in that moment I saw how I had clung to my dead brother for years, how I had been preoccupied with him, how I had pretended he was with me and had held on to him for dear life instead of fully living alone without him. It was a frightening moment.

I asked Jim what would happen to me if I said good-bye to David, imagining that a crash of thunder or some other frightening phenomenon would occur. Jim calmly said he did not know what would happen, that I would have to risk finding that out for myself by saying good-bye.

I hesitated further, and Jim said, "Perhaps you aren't ready." I heard that as a challenge. I imagined Jim thought I was too immature or too gutless to say good-bye. I said, "I want to be ready now," and then I turned to the empty chair that represented my brother and said, "Good-bye, David."

To my amazement nothing happened at all, neither the anticipated thunder nor any special feeling inside of me. I told Jim I felt empty, that I was surprised not to have more emotion in my dreaded good-bye. Jim said, "Try this. Say 'Good-bye, David' and then 'Hello, World.' "

I silently reflected that Jim's suggestion sounded crazy. However, since I had agreed to take the further risk, I did as he suggested and said, "Good-bye, David. Hello, World." I looked up at the group of people sitting in a circle around me, who had not existed for me up to that moment. I saw tears streaming down many of their faces as I said, "Hello, World." I jumped up and ran over to look at them more closely, to touch their tears. I was deeply moved to have so many people crying for me and with me. Then I experienced a joy I had never known before. I felt alive in a beautiful world of loving people. Alive was wonderful!

That moment was a turning point in my life. After fourteen years of grieving, I had faced painful, formerly unacceptable feelings, said good-bye to my brother, and fully rejoined the living. My chronic depression dissipated. My life has become better and better ever since.

As is evident from my own experience with finishing, one reason we do not fully finish with grief is that we might have to face aspects of ourselves we prefer to avoid. Because we tell ourselves we should not feel certain feelings, like anger, we try valiantly to suppress our unacceptable feelings. Often it is the part of us that we call "childish" or "selfish" that is struggling most with the loss. The child in each of us usually has the hardest time coping with suffering such as grief. Willingness to finish, then, involves allowing some of our less acceptable feelings to emerge and facing less mature and sometimes less attractive aspects of ourselves.

Experienced from the inside, this is the most profound finishing I can report. However, I have since been the facilitator of many finishings, each of which was a unique experience. The sharings of others' finishings are the highest moments of my professional career.

The following, an unusual, dramatic finishing, points up the steps a young woman took to let go of her dead mother. Sally felt abandoned at age ten when her mother died. The loss of a boyfriend almost twenty years later re-created all her old unfinished feelings of grief and abandonment from her mother's death. This was the reason she came for therapy.

To face her unfinished business with her mother, Sally agreed to have a dialogue, imagining her mother sitting in front of her. First, she expressed her sorrow at losing her mother. She cried profusely. Then I asked her to tell her mother she was angry at her for dying. More feelings rushed forth. She told her mother she was angry at being left so young to cope for herself, that her whole life had changed after her mother's death, that her father had withdrawn from her, and that she had no one to share her grief.

After this long, intense dialogue, where Sally seemed to release her feelings fully, I asked if she was willing now to say goodbye to her mother. She looked at me aghast and said, "No!" Then she expressed her fears of being a "motherless child," alone and abandoned. Sally confessed that to avoid feeling abandoned she had pretended her mother had been with her for the past eighteen years. Letting go of her mother was too terrifying to imagine.

Next, Sally tried pretending her imaginary mother was at her side, then switched and imagined herself alone. To experience each state fully, she went back and forth between the two. At first she felt too frightened to be alone, so she came up with a compromise for those times. She had a favorite velvet box, and she imagined she had put her mother in that box, which she would open only when she felt scared and needy. The velvet box, a startling and unusual metaphor, was Sally's way of offering herself an alternative to letting go of her mother completely. At this point, a change was beginning, for now Sally was making her mother less important, smaller, and apart from herself, if not yet absent.

As Sally continued in the therapy experiment with the velvet box, she suddenly realized that she had a choice as to whether to hold on to or let go of her mother. She had been so fixated on hanging on to her mother that she had seen no other choice. To check out if she was ready to let go, I asked her to imagine giving me the velvet box. She gave me the box freely. The symbolic letting-go felt good to her. She decided she did not want it back. With that decisive act she felt relieved, strong, proud of herself. We both knew she was finished. As she later regained her trust in others and established meaningful relationships, we knew the finishing was complete and effective.

Sally's resistance to letting go is probably familiar to all of us. Because letting go and saying good-bye all at once were so hard for Sally, we eased her into finishing with her mother step by step. Some people can take the action of finishing all at once, while others slowly work their way toward completion. We do not necessarily react to every finishing in our own lives in the same way either.

Another client who worked with me on the death of a mother finished in quite a different way. Steve's mother had died after a two-year illness with cancer, when Steve was thirteen. He felt he had had every opportunity to express his feelings and work them through directly with his mother, so open had they been about her death with one another. Yet Steve still grieved ten years later. When I suggested he start a dialogue with his mother, Steve began, "I still feel unfinished with you." He then expressed appreciations and resentments, but all his feelings seemed familiar to him. I suggested that he start a sentence with "I wish," to see if that was his unfinished business. Soon Steve was sobbing, as he expressed his deepest feeling: "I wish you had told me you loved me before you died." This seemed a terrible dilemma to Steve, wanting the impossible, to hear words from a dead person, yet that is exactly what is often incomplete.

I suggested that Steve sit in the chair where he had originally placed his mother, that he pretend to *be* his mother and respond accordingly. Speaking for his mother, Steve said many loving things, expressing her pride in Steve's handling of the loss as well as in his achievements in life. As his mother, Steve said, "I love you." Even though he had said it for his mother, Steve felt deeply that the sentiment was true. He was satisfied, and felt relief and a sense of completion with his mother. Within months of this therapeutic work, he fell in love with a woman for the first time and eventually married her.

A few years ago I did an experimental workshop for the Gestalt Institute of Phoenix, Arizona, entitled "A Workshop in Saying Good-bye." A dramatic finishing was done in that workshop by Ruth, a sixty-year-old woman whose husband had died two years earlier following a long illness. Ruth felt complete emotionally with her husband, both from having shared so many of her feelings with him and from having helped him die. But she felt compelled to keep their home exactly as he would have liked it, including keeping all his belongings as they were when he was alive. She felt enormous guilt whenever she considered rearranging or getting rid of any household item. She felt even worse whenever she thought of letting go of his belongings.

I suggested she share her dilemma in a dialogue aloud, imagining her husband sitting opposite her in an empty chair. Very shortly what emerged was that since her husband had bought her everything she now owned, she felt their belongings were still his, not hers. She seemed to want his permission to move or dispose of any of them. Ruth played the role of her husband and gave herself that permission. "He" went on to tell Ruth to make a full life for herself, to develop a career, to learn to make her own money if she chose, and even to remarry if that was her wish. The group cried as she spoke for her husband and said, "Ruthie, I am dead and you are alive. I want you to live as fully as you can. Live your life *your* way now."

This finishing demonstrates how we keep ourselves stuck, when we try to keep ourselves, our belongings, or our lives as they were before the loved one died. Ruth was able to see her situation more objectively by playing the role of her husband, and then she could change.

In that same workshop was Margery, whose young husband had committed suicide four years earlier. Whenever she began to speak about Brad or his death, Margery cried profusely. She felt abandoned and punished by his choosing suicide. Survivors usually experience suicide as a very angry act, no matter what the deceased's true intent was. Most prominent for Margery was her guilt that she had not found a way to save Brad, not bettered his life, so that he would be alive now.

In the dialogue with Brad that followed, I suggested that Margery first express all this guilt and sorrow. Later I asked her to imagine "being" her husband to tell her why he had committed suicide. As Brad, she expressed his pain, how he saw himself as a total failure and was unwilling to try any more or to go on with his life. He told her he wanted to die, and that there was no way she could have kept him alive. This provoked others in the group to talk about times when no one could help them with their despair. Eventually Margery came to terms with the critical issue that only Brad could be responsible for keeping himself alive. She knew now that she could not have changed his life. She knew more deeply how responsible she was for making a good life for herself. What had once been an intellectual idea became truth for Margery.

I have said that it is natural when loved ones die to be plagued with "if onlys" about their life and death. Often, as in the example of Margery, it is worthwhile to explore such "if onlys" in depth in a dialogue with the deceased to confirm for ourselves the truth that one cannot reverse the course of death and dying. The wish to reverse reality and the inability to accept the truth of death seem, however, to be the places in the grieving process in which we are most apt to become stuck.

Difficulty accepting the reality of death can also plague the professional who works with death and dying regularly. A colleague, Elaine, came to me for therapy months after one of her patients died. Struggling with guilt because she had not realized the patient was dying, Elaine said, "If only I had known, maybe I could have saved her." Since then, without being aware of the reason for her new symptom, Elaine had suffered a great deal of anxiety about dying herself, especially when she was alone at night.

I suggested that Elaine put her patient in a chair opposite herself and express her grief. Elaine sobbed deeply. She shared her sense of loss and how she could not forgive herself. I suggested she then change chairs and respond for the patient, which led her to say, "Of course I forgive you. You are not in any way responsible for my death. It was my time to die." Since her patient didn't blame her, my colleague could forgive herself. Elaine reported sleeping well from that night on, for the first time in the months since the patient had died.

The missing link in finishing with grief is often forgiveness. Sometimes we cannot forgive another, but we human beings are slowest to forgive ourselves. We also tend to take on responsibility for life-and-death matters that are not in our hands.

The issue of feeling responsible for another's death came up dramatically when Joyce's husband died of a heart attack twenty-four hours after they had had a fight. Joyce was flooded with "if onlys." She berated herself for fighting, for her anger, for expressing her unmet needs to her husband, for not knowing he might die. He had never had heart trouble before. More complicating for Joyce was the fact that they were fighting about whether to stay together or not. Joyce had been very ambivalent about staying in this marriage. Now she was torn with grief and resentment. Several weeks after her husband's death, Joyce expressed these feelings in a dialogue with him. As she played the role of her dead husband, "he" told her that he did not want to live any longer, that he had chosen to die. This made her very angry. She told him she felt he had "copped out" on her, on their children, on his life, and on working out their problems together. She told him she was angry that he had abandoned her emotionally and financially. Only after she had expressed all her anger did she voice regret that she did not let herself fully love him or acknowledge his love for her. After that she said she felt relieved of the relationship and "free." She was finished.

In most finishings there is some appreciation expressed to the deceased, whether it is acknowledged or not. Usually the survivor expresses appreciation at learning or growing from the experience of loss. In Joyce's case, the appreciation came from being free of the problems within the relationship with the deceased. This sometimes startling discovery often comes after the breakup of an intimate relationship, but not necessarily when a loved one dies. A person in the throes of grieving can find it hard to imagine that there is anything to appreciate. However, there is always some appreciation, which we might be more willing to admit in time, as shown by the following dramatic example.

During a professional Gestalt therapy workshop several years ago, Jack worked on his grief that his apartment building had burned down a month before. Jack's nearly finished doctoral thesis, which he had worked on at night for seven years while holding a full-time job, had been destroyed in the fire. Everyone in the group cried while listening to Jack express his pain at the loss of so much of his life's work. The therapist encouraged Jack to express his rage at the fire aloud.

After that, to my surprise, the therapist suggested, "Now express your appreciation to the fire." Many of us gasped. Jack paused for a moment and then said, "I am glad you burned my thesis. I hated it. It was something I designed seven years ago that no longer fits me or my interests. Now I will write a different thesis, which will be much easier, with all I have learned since." Within a few years I heard that Jack's friends were giving a party to celebrate his being awarded the doctorate in psychology.

In one Gestalt therapy workshop, after I had discussed the concept of finishing, Susan expressed feeling unfinished with her first husband, who had died at age twenty-five, twenty years earlier. Although she had since remarried and been divorced, the feeling of being unfinished with him still plagued her. After she had an imaginary dialogue with her dead husband, we both felt baffled at the absence of any deep emotions. Sometimes people are so blocked that they withhold feelings, even with deep provocation, but that did not seem to be the case with Susan.

At my suggestion, Susan sat in her husband's "chair" so that she could speak for him. When he was asked what his feelings were about saying good-bye, with a great rush of emotion "he" told her never to say good-bye to him and never to love another man. The intensity of emotion shocked both Susan and me. Susan said she felt as if he were really speaking through her. She changed from one chair to the other as "they" argued back and forth. "His" urgency and need for her felt real. Susan finally resolved the conflict within her by telling him she would be with him again in an afterlife or another life. "He" seemed to relent with this promise to reunite with him in the future, and they said good-bye. It was a powerful experience. Susan was deeply affected by this sensing of her husband's attachment to her. She felt she was filled with her dead husband's energy, so present did he seem to her in that dialogue. Afterward she was relieved and relaxed. She felt a completion of that old relationship.

Recently a client named Nan asked me to do a family session for her and her three brothers, all of whom needed to grieve and finish with their father, who had died a year earlier. At the time of their father's death, each sibling had withdrawn inside and gone his or her separate way. None had fully grieved. The closeness among them had seemed to wane since, as well.

The five of us came from different cities to hold this session.

The clients shared memories of their father; they expressed their reactions to their roles in the family, their childhood memories, their reactions to one another, and then, finally, their sorrow, anger, and grief at the loss of their father. They each carried a lot of unfinished childhood business, particularly related to their father. Many discoveries, insights, surprises, feelings, and tears were shared. Much warmth, relief, and intimacy followed. The oldest brother encouraged us to enjoy ourselves after this intense session, and the five of us spent the evening at Disneyland. It was a great pleasure to be light and playful after the intensity of the therapy earlier that day. For me, it was rare and extraordinary working with several members of a family at one time to finish with grief. From this important sharing together, each felt a great clearing, relief, and healing.

There are other ways to complete grief besides the Gestalt therapy method, of course. Recently a client told me how she had finished with her dead nephew. Shortly after his death, she wrote him a letter in which she expressed all her feelings about him, their relationship, his family, and her reactions to his death. Then she realized that he was only four years old and unable to read, so she read the completed letter aloud, as if the little boy were in hearing distance. This woman had spontaneously created her own way of finishing.

Years ago, before I was a Gestalt therapist, I took part in a lengthy finishing with Laura, age twenty-three, who had become psychotic after an abortion. She was so consumed with guilt that she had lost her sense of reality. But once we thoroughly explored the source of her guilt, she recovered within a few months.

Laura's was an unusual story. When she was six, her father had died in an accident. She had been his favorite, and she felt he was the only one who loved her. Her sense of loss was enormous. From then on she felt like Cinderella, lost, lonely, and badly treated by her mother and older sister. After seeing her mother talking to her father's grave, she got the idea of talking with her father regularly too. She always kept his photograph nearby and talked to it. She discussed all her feelings with "him," and eventually all her decisions as well. She imagined his responses and meticulously followed what she thought were his ideas about how she should live her life.

She felt she had lived up to her father's expectations, until she had her first sexual experience as an unmarried woman of twenty-three. She was sure he did not approve. Guilt began to consume her. Naïve about birth control, she became pregnant. She saw the pregnancy as her punishment for unmarried sex. Her religious background did not favor abortion. However, the man who impregnated her had moved away with no intention of seeing her again. A friend encouraged Laura to have an abortion and supported her through the process.

Upon awakening from anesthesia after the abortion, Laura imagined seeing her father looking down on her from above her hospital bed. First she experienced terror, then consuming guilt, and then severe depression. This was her first actual vision of her father. After this she lost her sense of reality and came for psychiatric help.

In therapy we discovered together that making her dead father a real person seemed a necessity for Laura to survive her seemingly Cinderella-like childhood. She nourished herself with thoughts of her father, fantasies which helped her endure feeling otherwise unloved. For Laura, finishing was a long, arduous process because of the enormity of her fears of letting go. Mainly she feared that without her imaginary father she would not survive. She feared she would not know how to function without his "guidance." And she feared she would make more terrible mistakes in living. To help her let go of her father, I talked her through every step of the way, much as one imagines talking to a potential suicide who is standing on a dangerous ledge. At the same time, we worked together to help her develop a more realistic support system in her life, such as friends, a job, a home, and social activities, so that she would not feel so much in need of the support of a dead man.

Only after Laura had created a supportive group of friends would she consider actually letting go of her imaginary father. Since we had talked endlessly about letting go, the actual finishing with her father was not dramatic. We set a date for her good-bye in advance, much as one might do to get rid of a habit. When the day came, she kept her agreement and said good-bye to her father aloud. Her tears had been shed earlier. Now there were none. She felt proud of herself and relieved that she had said good-bye at last. The happy ending is that this young woman, who had always had so much trouble with closeness and trust, made several lasting friends and married happily within a couple of years of that finishing.

The techniques described here for finishing with loss are applicable to any kind of resolution one needs to make. For example, Dorothy gave birth to a child with a facial defect. When she first saw him, she was horrified and hoped he would not survive. Later she was overwhelmed with guilt that she had wished her now-beloved baby dead. I suggested that Dorothy have a dialogue aloud, imagining that she was talking to the baby in a chair opposite herself and telling him the truth of her original feelings as well as how she felt now. She grieved. She expressed her sorrow, her guilt, her disappointment, and her anger. Then she relaxed and felt relieved and accepting of her feelings. She told him how much she loved him and that she would have the defect surgically repaired when he was older. After that she felt free to delight in her new baby.

Another example is that of Barbara, whose husband, Robert, had suffered a severe life-threatening illness from which he had recovered. Her gratitude at his recovery led her to deny her experience with his illness. In a therapy session she was reminded of the many days and nights of anguish before he recovered. I suggested that she have a dialogue, imagining her husband in front of her and telling him in this way, rather than in reality, what the experience of his illness was like for her. She told him of her fears, of how hard it was to work full-time and then drive the many miles to the hospital daily, of how hard it was to handle his distraught parents, who leaned on her throughout his illness, and of how alone she felt in coping. She told him how angry she was, that she was too young to have such responsibility at a time in her life when she wanted to have fun and play. She stopped when she could think of no more to say. Several weeks later she told me she had stopped thinking about her husband's illness. Only then did she realize that she had thought about that experience daily. She knew she was finished when all thoughts about his illness disappeared.

There are many ways to finish. However, almost everyone needs to express feelings or to ruminate enough after a loss to be able to let go of the person or the experience. One friend told me of her client, a man whose son had died of leukemia. The father had been working on getting out all his feelings when one day he came to his therapist and said, "I have been de-griefed." How he knew, he said, was that "Now I can think about my son and enjoy it," rather than experience pain.

WHEN ARE WE FINISHED?

How do we know when we are finished? Usually we can be sure if we take plenty of time to explore and express our feelings, and if we experience some kind of emotional release or a change in attitude after that. Our own physical and emotional health can testify to our finishing, especially if we had been plagued with symptoms. We are finished when our grief feelings seem dissipated, when we can think of the loss or the loved one without pain, and when we can incorporate the fact of death into our lives. Time is one of the most important ingredients of healing. Hence, we may have a deep emotional release a month or so after a loved one dies and still not be quite finished getting used to the absence of the loved one from our lives.

My clients' experiences were similar to mine. I knew I had finished with my brother when I stopped thinking about him so frequently and when thoughts of him did not cause me any particular emotions or reactions. Of course, I would never forget him. I was particularly aware that I had let go when I stopped dreaming frequently about him. Dreams can be signals of our unfinished business, and for some people they may be a barometer of our working something through to completion. Similarly, frequent painful thoughts of the deceased are a strong indication that we still are unfinished.

In summary, many of us are unable to complete our grief work when the loved one is alive or immediately after death occurs. Hence, after a loss we are left with many feelings that block us from fully living in the present and from fully enjoying our lives. Our inability to say good-bye keeps us from letting go, often long after the loss has occurred. In its directness, the Gestalt therapy method of finishing can enable us to finish sooner and more fully than any other method I know.

Finishing is essential if we are to live enriched, satisfying lives. What is unfinished pulls on us still, takes up our energy, and thus reduces our capacity for living. It would be ideal if we could be fully authentic and stay current in every one of our relationships; that is, share ourselves and our feelings openly and honestly, so that we would not have such backlogs of unfinished business when we have to say good-bye. Finishing, which involves the willingness to experience and express feelings fully, usually leads to a release of feelings, after which a shift in perspective and then resolution occurs. Finished, one feels free, relieved, peaceful, energized, even joyous, with the flood of new energy from within. Finished, we are free to remember and to love without pain, sorrow, or regret.

Facing the crisis of a loved one's death is often a major turning point in our lives. In the next two chapters we will look at how a loss can affect our decisions about our lives and how it can be a stepping-stone to transforming our lives.

13

Loss as a Turning Point

And shall it be said that
my eve was in truth my dawn?
　　　　—The Prophet

Whenever we are affected by a trauma, such as a death, we make some kinds of decisions or resolutions about our lives. Often these decisions, made under stress, profoundly affect our future. The critical resolution might be a thought we keep to ourselves or a statement we make to others. Sometimes the resolution is simply forgotten after the intensity of the crisis wears off. We may not be aware of our decisions because they were not made consciously.

Under the stress of loss, we may make statements such as "I will never love again" or other kinds of positive or negative "never again" resolutions. Sometimes we vow future growth for ourselves, such as "Next time I'll learn to cope with . . ." or "When I grow up, I'll . . ." We promise to do something, like my decision in 1956 to write a book dedicated to my dead brother. We may also resign ourselves to failure, with such thoughts as "I cannot overcome my sorrow" or "I will give up" or "I won't try again."

The resolutions we make during a loss or other crisis have great impact, because these are times when we are particularly vulnerable and therefore more suggestible. Thus the decisions we make become affirmations or assertions of truth or fact, whether true or not. As we have seen, psychologists call such resolutions or affirmations "self-fulfilling prophecies." In other words, our thoughts are powerful; thoughts can create our reality.

It is critically important, therefore, that we examine and acknowledge our thoughts so that we may create positive rather than negative realities for ourselves. We might also delay decision-making until the crisis we are facing passes. In this chapter are examples of how people created their realities from resolutions made after the death of a loved one. Later on I will describe the way to consciously design such resolutions or affirmations.

From extensive interviewing of people who have suffered losses, I find that people often are not conscious of any decisions they might have made for themselves when their loved ones died. I believe we make such decisions whether we are conscious of doing so or not. It is my hope that I can make readers conscious of this kind of decision-making and provoke them to remember past resolutions after encountering an important loss. Such recall can be an important tool in understanding ourselves.

The most dramatic resolution was shared with me by Maria, a client who had recurrent breast cancer. She described herself before her illness as a woman who frequently contemplated suicide as a way to get out of her life. Then one day her depressed lover committed suicide. She was shocked and overwhelmed, both by the enormity of her loss and by the fact that he had taken his own life. She thought a lot then about the devastating effects of suicide on surviving loved ones. After that, she said to herself, "I will never commit suicide and hurt my family. It's not like dying of cancer where everyone loves you and feels sorry for you." Two years later when she developed cancer, she remembered—to her horror—those earlier thoughts.

As noted earlier, researchers are discovering how frequently the loss of a loved one precedes the onset of disease, by weeks, months, or a few years. This has often been observed in the development of cancer. Carl and Stephanie Simonton, in their book *Getting Well Again*, discuss at length the historical evidence connecting emotional factors such as the suffering of a loss with the onset of cancer. The Simontons note that prior to the onset of cancer their clients "often . . . recall wishing they were dead or feeling hopeless and thinking that death was the only way out."

The most common resolution after the loss of a loved one is "I will never love again" or "I will never love wholeheartedly again." I am sure we have all seen widows or widowers who seem to withdraw their lovingness from the world after the death of a spouse. A most dramatic example was a buoyant, beautiful fifty-year-old woman whose husband had died while they were vacationing together. She returned home and literally shriveled up, withdrew, and aged, in her belief that she would never love again. Similarly, I knew a very angry woman years ago in a clinic where we both worked who spent her days snarling at patients and staff alike. A colleague told me she had been this way ever since her only child had died a few years before. Clearly her message to the world, expressed through her anger, was "I will never love anyone again."

A more subtle example of the decision "I will never love again" is the case of Dick, whose young wife died of cancer. Together they had faced her dying. Dick felt he had worked through much of his grief in talking with his wife before her death. After she died he felt strong; he handled their children, their friends, her things, and his life-style. But he got stuck in his belief that he had lost the one true love of his life. He thought he would never love again. That belief was in fact unfinished business, which he was not aware of. The "story" he told himself was that great love comes once in a lifetime. Hence, when he married again, he did not expect love, and he lived out a self-fulfilling prophecy that caused him even more grief. Several years after his second marriage, Dick came to me for therapy because of severe and chronic depression. What we discovered was that he had settled for much less in life than he wanted, because of his "I will never love again" resolution. He subsequently left his second marriage and eventually fell in love again.

It is important to note here how much idealization of the deceased might affect the kinds of decisions we make about our lives. There is always the tendency, especially at first, to idealize a dead loved one. Loss sometimes makes us see perfection where it did not really exist. It is natural to want to shut off the bad memories, or the idea of imperfections in the loved one, and to remember only the good traits or times. Unfortunately, this process can lead us to cling to something that was not real in the first place, such as "He was such a perfect husband, I'll never find another like him." This false belief makes the people in our lives look like midgets in comparison with the giant who has died. Such idealization can prevent us from creating new relationships for ourselves. We then deny the important fact that if we were capable of creating this deep, special love relationship with the deceased, we know how to create such a relationship with a new love.

Many of us think that "I will never love again" is a fitting memorial to our dead loved one. We imagine that we are telling the deceased how special, how loved, how irreplaceable in our lives he or she is. Of course, the loved one was unique and special, but this denial of self is a misguided way to express love. Imagine how the deceased would look at the choice never to love again. Who would ever want to doom a surviving loved one to only memories and loneliness for the rest of their lives? Giving up living and loving is not a fitting memorial to love.

The "I will never love again" resolution is very common after a loss. The pain of loss is so great, so hard to bear, that it is natural to think we can never tolerate such pain again. We imagine that not loving will protect us from that pain. However, in giving up the possibility of the pain of loss, we miss the chance for joy and all the other pleasures of loving.

There are many other kinds of "never again" decisions that a person may make at the time of a loss. For example, as an outgrowth of her mother's death, Donna resolved never again to trust anyone to tell her the truth. Only when Donna overheard a doctor telling her father that her mother would die within twenty-four hours did she know that her mother was seriously ill with cancer. Donna's resentment over the two years of pretending that her mother was recovering led her to conclude that she could trust no one to tell her the truth. The decision never to trust anyone again wreaked havoc in Donna's life. Many years after her mother died, she stopped this destructive programming of her life through psychotherapy.

When a loss is unexpected and shocking, we sometimes blame ourselves, unjustly, for being unprepared. Consciously or unconsciously, we may then put up our guard to prepare and defend against any eventuality. Such was the case with Lisa, age thirty, who felt unprepared for her husband's unexpected death from an illness. Lisa decided she would have to be tougher, more guarded, to fend off further tragedies. Unaware, Lisa changed from a soft, loving woman to a hardened, distrustful one.

When a loved one dies, people sometimes make unconscious resolutions that later become impossible to live with. The pressure of internal conflict created by such a resolution may bring it into consciousness. This had been Sara's experience when she came to me for psychotherapy. Sara was uneasy about feeling generally withdrawn and deadened. She experienced this as a sudden change, out of her control. When we explored her emotions together, we discovered that she was avoiding anger as a totally unacceptable feeling. Rather than be angry she would withdraw, and then she would feel detached and unreal. The root of her problem was that she had been angry at her husband shortly before he died of a heart attack. Because she felt responsible for his death, she resolved never to be angry again. She feared her anger would incur disastrous consequences. As children often do, Sara exaggerated her power in circumstances where in fact she was powerless. She was not conscious of making a decision but was suffering from her attempts at massive self-control. Her resolution never to get angry again was impossible for her to live with, as it would be for most of us. The pressure to control herself created internal havoc and distress. In order to resolve her conflict, it was necessary for her to forgive herself for having been angry at her husband, as well as to accept anger as a normal part of living.

The most negative of all decisions one can make when a loved one dies is to resolve to give up living. A friend told me a dramatic story of this kind about her mother-in-law, Mary. When Mary's husband died after a long battle with cancer, Mary did not want to live without him. It appears that on some level she had resolved to die. Each night before she fell asleep Mary methodically re-created her husband's illness in step-by-step detail. Thus, she fell asleep each night with vivid pictures of her husband, his illness, and his death. Within a year Mary developed cancer in exactly the same place that her husband had suffered this disease. She died within a matter of weeks. I believe that Mary created her reality, having resolved to die rather than live without her husband. Mary had picked bedtime, a particularly vulnerable and suggestible time, to re-create memories and to visualize illness and death for herself. Each of us has this same power to create our reality, which we can use for our own benefit or for our demise. Later in this chapter I will discuss more ways to use this power consciously in a positive way.

When the friend who told me the story of Mary read these words, she realized with amazement that after her mother-in-law had died in this way she herself had resolved never to love a man so much that she could not live without him. My friend, a widow, had felt cut off from loving for years without understanding the reason—until then.

Sometimes "never again" decisions can support our growth and life changes. Frequently after a loss I have heard people say something like "Never again will I hide my love from my family and friends." Not to have expressed our love before the loved one's death is a great sorrow to live with. It is a painful lesson that so many of us have to learn. Hence, many of us resolve never to withhold our deep feelings again.

After a loved one dies we may decide to live differently or to change or grow in some specific way. We may try to live more fully, especially when we feel the deceased was cut short from a full life. Some people develop new interests, even new careers, in response to a loss; many people quit smoking after the death of someone close. Sometimes we decide to emulate some behavior of the deceased. This is frequently true in children who lose an admired parent or grandparent. Many of us have fashioned our careers or our interests to be like those of someone we love who has died.

Or we may want to be different from the person who died. Several young women whose mothers died before the young women were grown decided not to be seemingly unhappy house-wives, as their mothers had been, but to establish meaningful careers for themselves as adults. There are many examples in these pages of people who made changes in themselves or their lives after the death of a loved one. Frequently people become more independent after a loss, realizing more of their own poten-tial. Or they may make major life changes or small personality changes in response to the death of a loved one. Examples of some of the transformations of people and their lives will be found in chapter 14.

When my psychiatrist, Mel Boigon, died during our work to-gether, I decided not only to handle his death well but also to cope well with any future losses in my life. I felt this would be the greatest tribute to his helping me come to terms with my brother's death. Mel's death helped me accept death as a fact of life rather than as a victimization of myself. I felt as if I had "grown up" when I made that resolution.

Widows of all ages have told me how they resolved, once they were on their own, to "grow up" and to function successfully and independently. And a widower with young children resolved to run his home and raise his children, tasks formerly left to his wife, all of which gave him a great sense of satisfaction in his own growth. Several young people have told me of feeling forced to "grow up" after the death of a parent. Most resolved successfully to be competent beyond their years.

A profound decision in coping with the death of a loved one is to work with others suffering a loss. Recently self-help groups of the formerly bereaved have sprung up around the country to help people in mourning. Many of the people I know in the helping professions, such as social workers, psychologists, and physicians, resolved to help others because of a death earlier in their lives. Some were moved to make this decision because of someone who helped them. Others had felt such a strong need for help that they wanted to learn how to be a helper for others. Another woman I know found the trauma of her daughter's death in a car accident overwhelming and unbearable for many months. As she began to recover, she resolved to help other parents face the loss of a child. The resolve to help, to assist humanity in some way, is one of the most positive resolutions one can make after suffering a loss.

Since most of us usually make some kind of decision or resolution at the time of a major life crisis, it is worthwhile for each of us to be conscious of the resolution-making process. It might even be possible to consider in advance of life's crises the decisions we might make for ourselves. I have heard people say, "If my mother ever dies" or "If I ever lost my child (wife, husband, etc.)" as if programming their behavior in advance. With knowledge we might *learn* to create positive rather than negative resolutions for ourselves. Instead of "I'll never again . . ." we might consider sentences that start with "From now on I want to . . ." Making a positive decision instead of a negative one when confronting a life crisis could make all the difference in how we cope as well as in how we go on with our lives.

We also tend to see ourselves in fixed ways, remembering how we coped or failed to cope in the past instead of seeing ourselves as fresh, able, and perhaps now skilled in coping. By relying on old memories of ourselves, we are apt to overlook our own change and growth as a result of these past experiences.

To give us some ideas of how to create positive realities for ourselves, here are some positive affirmations people have made at the times of losses in their lives, together with some examples of positive statements we might make.

I have the courage to go through this experience.

I grow from adversity.

I am strong.

I am strong enough to cope.

I can overcome my sorrow.

I will finish with my grief and build a new life.

From now on I will share all my loving feelings.

From now on I will have no unfinished business with my loved ones.

From now on I intend to be patient (persevering, understanding, honest, open, etc.).

From now on I intend to live my life to the fullest.

Using affirmations for personal growth is discussed at length in chapter 11. Affirmations are the beginning of creating the changes we desire. If, for example, I simply consider the option of having courage or strength or independence or whatever it is that I want, I am already feeding myself a positive idea that has the potential to become reality. It seems worthwhile to repeat here the beautiful example given me by my friend Tom. When he discovered that he had lung cancer, he was of course frightened, but he wanted to appear courageous to the woman he loved, so he *pretended* to have courage. Soon he found that he was in fact being courageous. It is as if Tom made himself wear shoes a size too large. From there he succeeded in fitting himself to the shoes he wanted to wear.

Previewing possibilities helps us to reach out, to expand, and to grow. Previewing means taking the opportunity in advance to imagine what is possible. One way to preview is to picture ourselves as having the quality or qualities we desire. Another way is to ask ourselves what we would be like if we had the courage (or whatever the quality is), or how we imagine a courageous (or strong or whatever) person would cope. Or we can try to remember someone we have known who behaved in a way that we admire and would like to emulate. Imagining ourselves coping better or differently is often the beginning of change. All of us have small pictures of ourselves that are limited, as well as old ideas of how we behave in the world. We need also to develop larger pictures of ourselves, pictures we might grow to fit.

Another way to expand our sense of ourselves is visualization. Visualizations are pictures we create in our own minds to change or enhance a situation. Some of us adapt more readily to visualizing change than others.

The visualization technique is simple. First, we picture ourselves as we want to be, as if we are already changed or expanded in the new way we desire. If we wish, we can meditate or relax in order to picture ourselves as this new person. We might do visualizations before we go to bed each night and as we rise each morning, for those are times when we are often more sensitive and suggestible.

Picturing ourselves as we would like to be is a way to make real in our mind's eye the new idea we have for ourselves. By so picturing ourselves, we act as if the change has already been accomplished. Whenever a situation in life appears as if it might be hard for us, we might in advance picture ourselves as coping well. This technique can work for any situation in our lives, new or old, familiar or unfamiliar.

Since we all make important decisions or resolutions under the stress of loss, we need to look at the resolutions we may have made in the past. They can be reversed, if we can only become aware of them. The information in this chapter can also help us prepare ourselves for future losses. How would we like to respond to loss in our lives? There seems to me no greater memorial to loved ones who have died than using their deaths to propel ourselves to grow and to live our own lives in some better way. The more we take responsibility for creating our own lives effectively, the more rewarding and satisfying our lives will be. Chapter 14 gives examples of some ways people have enhanced, expanded, and transformed their lives.

14
Transformation

And the treasure of your infinite depths
would be revealed to your eyes.
—The Prophet

When a loved one dies we are confronted with a profound challenge. We can either give up or grow from the experience. We can succumb to adversity or use adversity to transform our lives. "We are infinitely strong and endlessly able to start our journey of evolvement again. It is the true miracle of life that you can brutalize it, tear it apart, and still it survives."

The death of a loved one is so painful an experience that it is often the turning point in the life of the survivor. Whoever we were, whatever we believed, however we lived—all are open to question and doubt. So deeply are we moved by the impact of severing a love relationship that we are bound to change in some way. Our perspective on life is altered, sometimes profoundly. Facing a death induces us to see as if through new eyes. Life may look more dangerous, fragile, or unpredictible now, or instead life may seem more delineated, more challenging, or more to be cherished.

Our feelings too may change after the death of a loved one. Our pain can provoke us to be bitter, angry, disappointed—even to consider quitting. Or pain can mobilize us to live, risk, experiment, and experience. Pain can be the teacher that arouses us to discover our true feelings and to question and search for answers. From our pain we can learn and grow.

Our relationships also change after a loved one dies. Some of us move closer to remaining loved ones, knowing how transient and precious our time is together. Others move away and with-draw rather than again risk sorrow, regret, or pain.

Loss can launch the survivor into a new life, for with loss come many changes and adjustments. Until we experience a significant loss, we may be unaware of life, death, or feelings, as if living in a protective cocoon. The death of a loved one can suddenly transport us to new ground, releasing us to leave the cocoon and become a butterfly. Because of a loss, we may change our behavior, our values, our attitudes, our way of living, even our appearance. We may suddenly be propelled to take a totally new course of action, or we may commit ourselves more intensely to the course we had already chosen.

Spiritual transformation also may occur after the death of a loved one. Even if we have been nonbelievers, many of us begin to search for answers to such questions as Why are we here? What is the purpose of life? What is death? What follows life? For some of us, seeking answers leads us to a spiritual path and to a developing or deepening of our beliefs. Death leads some of us to see life in a context that is larger than that which is visible and concrete. We find a larger purpose, a sense of God, a belief in an afterlife, and the transcendence of the spirit beyond the body, beyond this lifetime. Some of us tune in to a sense of divine guidance that transforms our whole way of being in the world.

Grief, like manure, is meaningless until we learn how to use it. We use manure to grow beautiful flowers or delicious food. Similarly, we need to make something good come from our grief. Making our grief meaningful can be the antidote to despair and suffering as well as the stepping-stone to personal growth and achievement. We each must find our own meanings in order to transform our suffering into something of value. "At any moment, man must decide for better or for worse, what will be the monument to his existence."

Each of us can be a creative survivor. We can choose to turn great personal tragedy into life-affirming action or personal change. The more we reach toward life, instead of withdrawing into our tragedy, and the more we aim for achievement or accomplishment, the more we expand our own possibilities. To transform ourselves does not mean to become something we are not, but to expand ourselves to our farthest reaches, to achieve our greatest potential. It is from reaching beyond ourselves, beyond our sorrow, that we are transformed.

As survivors we may wonder, Why me? Why am I alive, while the other is dead? Often we see no wisdom in our survival. Some of us stay unhappily immobile, bewildered by being alive. The process that follows for others of us is that, mystified by our survival, we want our lives to be full of meaning to justify our being spared death. We then begin to create our own meaning, which can be the prerequisite to personality change or growth, to a change in our lives, or even to profound accomplishment. We act in order to enhance the life we have been given. It is not simply guilt that propels us to take leaps in our lives but, even more, a deep, sometimes unconscious, wish to make ourselves worthy of survival.

After my brother died I felt for the first time the pull to live a life of meaning. From being a frivolous teenager when he died, I moved from wanting to just party and play to wanting to be of value, to justify my own existence. To me a meaningful life meant being of service to others, so I went on to college and graduate school with that goal in mind. In choosing this path, I had already begun to transform myself, but I was conscious of my transformation only in retrospect, years later. Even after I had become a therapist and had been helping others for several years, I still ached for more, still doubted the value of my existence. As I developed deeper vision and more perspective, the ache in me began to subside. However, the satisfaction of my wish for meaning culminated in my writing this book, which I hoped might spare many the endless suffering of grief.

Elisabeth Kübler-Ross, born a two-pound triplet, said of her own life, "I had the feeling that I had to prove all my life that even a two-pound nothing—that I had to work really hard, like some blind people think that they have to work ten times as hard to keep a job. I had to prove very hard that I was worth living." That fact, combined with her reaction to the Second World War, led Kübler-Ross to her work on death and dying. After the war she said, "I personally saw the concentration camps. I personally saw trainloads of baby shoes, trainloads of human hair from the victims of the concentration camps taken to Germany to make pillows. When you smell the concentration camps with your own nose, when you see the crematoriums, when you're very young as I was . . . you will never, ever be the same." These experiences transformed Kübler-Ross from a typical survivor into one of the most influential and important humanists of our time. Her work has been instrumental in effecting changes for thousands and has helped create more humanity in our dealings with death and dying.

Many people from what I earlier called the "secret society" of mourners go on from grief to become counselors, therapists, physicians, and healers for other suffering souls. Out of loss experiences, many go on to serve, to teach, to be compassionate helpers, to enable others to enhance their lives. This seems to be a frequently chosen path of transformation after a loss experience. Hence, one who was fearful of death and dying may become a fearless counselor to the dying or grief-stricken after a loved one dies. One to whom pain seemed insurmountable chooses work that aims to alleviate human suffering. A parent who thought he could not survive the anguish of his own child's death works with dying children or grief-stricken parents. Peter Koestenbaum described the transformation of a father whose son was killed by a drunk driver. This father drove across California with his son's battered car on a trailer, agitating for stricter laws against drunk driving. His single-minded efforts helped establish some of the nation's strictest legislation against drunk driving in California. Another dramatic example of this kind of person was Betty, who faced her guilt-ridden years of incest only after her father's death. Betty now works with children and families who have suffered from incest. Betty-the-victim was transformed into Betty-the-helper.

Entertaining others is another kind of service that people choose after suffering a significant loss in their lives. This was dramatized in a *Time* magazine article on Jewish comedians. Although the Jewish population in the United States is only 3 percent, Jews comprise 80 percent of all American comedians. Psychologist Samuel Janus, interviewing many of these comedians, found that every one of them had experienced childhood tragedy and suffering. Most significant was how many of these comedians had lost an important loved one during childhood. These comedians transformed their pain into laughter and humor, bringing joy to others.

We are surrounded by inspiring survivors who have turned their lives around or dramatically changed or grown after suffering a significant loss. Our literature is filled with such examples, among whom are Anne Morrow Lindbergh and Catherine Marshall. Politically, women and men alike have been spurred on by childhood tragedy to achieve greatness. Abraham Lincoln and Eleanor Roosevelt are only two who come to mind. In the 1970s we saw Muriel Humphrey, a former housewife, competently take over her dead husband's Senate seat. Diane Kennedy Pike, widow of Bishop James Pike after only a few years of marriage, went on to write some deeply inspiring books about her own grief and to develop a program of spiritual-psychological help called "The Love Project." Peter Koestenbaum coined the term "ego transcending achievements," which aptly describes the work of many of these people.

One of the most profound transformations in our times is the restoration of the cities and survivors so badly devastated by the Second World War. Countries have not only recovered but are thriving now, years later. Many of the survivors are thriving as well. The victims of the Holocaust, who were faced with continual brutality and death and who lost most of their loved ones, have gone on to restore themselves and their lives. Some formed the foundation for the creation of the State of Israel. Israel's Prime Minister Menachem Begin, in the signing of the peace agreement with Egypt in March 1979, described Israel as a creation of survivors of the Holocaust.

It is my hope that these examples will inspire each of us to confront the sorrows in our lives and to move beyond our pain to enhance our lives in some way. I hope we will not each be tested so severely as to have to face war and disaster in our lifetime. However, each of us will have to face some loss. Though losing a loved one can be devastating, we each have to find a means to survive this experience; beyond survival is the possibility that we may grow or develop in some new way because of our loss. We may mature. We may deepen. We may create. We may serve, or teach, or entertain. We may appreciate our lives anew. Most of all, I hope each of us will learn to live *now,* to live fully, to live well. As Elisabeth Kübler-Ross has said so movingly:

> All the hardships that you face in life, all the tests and tribulations, all the nightmares, and all the losses, most people still view as curses, as punishments by God, as something negative. If you would only know that nothing that comes to you is negative. I mean *nothing.* All the trials and tribulations, and the biggest losses that you ever experience, things that make you say, "If I had known about this, I would never have been able to make it through," are gifts to you. It's like somebody had to—what do you call that when you make the hot iron into a tool?—you have to temper the iron. It is an opportunity that you are given to grow. That is the sole purpose of existence on this planet Earth. You will not grow if you sit in a beautiful flower garden, and somebody brings you gorgeous food on a silver platter. But you will grow if you are sick, if you are in pain, if you experience losses, and if you do not put your head in the sand, but take the pain and learn to accept it, not as a curse or a punishment, but as a gift to you with a very, very specific purpose.

PART FIVE

Self-Help

15

Breaking Through
Our Denial of Death

For life and death are one,
even as the river and the sea are one.
                    —The Prophet

Now that we have looked at the grief experience from many angles, we need to go back and look into ourselves. Since it is often our denial of death that prevents us from fully experiencing and completing our grief, we need to penetrate this denial. Of the many benefits we receive from breaking through our denial of death, the most important is the possibility of living life unafraid. Unafraid of death, we can live with more zeal and we can take more chances to achieve growth and enrichment. Unafraid of death, we can risk deeper, closer relationships. Unafraid of death, we can take life as something precious, not something ordinary. Then we have a greater chance of fulfilling whatever might be our destiny. When we break through our fears and resistances, we become more alive. When we face life courageously, unafraid, we feel more accomplished, wiser, and more powerful.

But how do we break through our denial of death? The first step is to want to face death squarely. Only then can we take action. Behaving as if we accept the reality of death can be the forerunner of truly feeling that acceptance. We might first read books on death and dying. We might discuss death openly with our intimates, parents, children, spouse, and friends. We can take the responsibility for writing a will. We can prepare our belongings and important papers for the eventuality of our demise. We can buy life insurance and health or accident insurance. We can confront death directly by talking with people who are dying, who are in the throes of grief, or who work every day with the dying. And we can examine our own attitudes about death and dying. Being open about all these issues will help us, and it can be a comfort and aid to our survivors as well.

WRITING A WILL

We can learn to write a valid will with the help of an attorney or by studying one of several books available on the subject. Writing a will is in itself an admission that we expect to die. A will is also a sign of our deep consideration for our loved ones and survivors. The process of will-writing may illuminate our feelings about life and help us to re-examine our values, attitudes, and relationships. This re-examination may lead to changing some aspect of life *now*. Writing a will can also help us examine our attachment to material possessions. It led me to realize that I want to give to people I love now, while I am alive. Kahlil Gibran writes in *The Prophet*, "Therefore give now, that the season of giving may be yours and not your inheritors'."

Each family member, regardless of age, might write a will, or wills might be a topic of discussion for the whole family. One way we deny death is by avoiding intimacy on death-related subjects with family and friends.

PREPARING BELONGINGS AND PAPERS

Another action that cuts through the denial of death is organizing our belongings and papers, thus assisting those loved ones who will someday have to dispose of them. This is a way both to prepare for death and to take responsibility for what we own, and it may result in a major reorganizing that will make our own lives easier. For example, I periodically sort anew and cast away books, papers, and clothing as a discipline for myself. This keeps me current on what I value and gives me an opportunity to give things away now.

We should also let loved ones know the details of how our will, finances, papers, and possessions are arranged. As a means of denying death we often keep this important information from those we love. Similarly, we can discuss with intimates our preferences for funeral, burial, cremation, donation of body parts, and so forth. Nowadays attorneys have a form called a "Living Will," wherein we can request that our life not be prolonged by machinery. In addition, telling the family attorney the location of important papers, safe-deposit boxes, insurance policies, and other such personal information is a helpful preparation for dying.

BUYING LIFE INSURANCE

Obtaining life insurance is another way of facing the possibility of death squarely and consciously. People often avoid life insurance out of denial or superstition. As a result, many a family has suffered severely the loss of a breadwinner who did not provide economic security for loved ones. By contrast, a client of mine was able to complete college and to support her family with insurance money, after her young husband's unexpected death.

DEALING DIRECTLY WITH DEATH AND DYING

Learning about death through direct experience is a profound way to confront reality. Talking with someone who is dying or with someone who has suffered a recent loss is often moving and illuminating. Without experience with death, we may have more fantasy than reality in our ideas about death and dying. Similarly, it is valuable to talk with people who deal directly with death and dying, people like morticians, hospital personnel, and physicians. Many of us feel ignorant and have many questions about death that can be answered if we will only ask.

Seeing death is a dramatic way to break through denial, but this is a frightening prospect for many of us. After the Jonestown massacre in Guyana, a radio newsman described how he was unable to rid himself of the sight and smell of death as the bodies lay decaying in the intense heat. Never again could he deny the existence of death. Lewis Thomas talks movingly about seeing death: "It is always a queer shock, part a sudden upwelling of grief, part unaccountable amazement. It is simply astounding to see an animal dead on the highway. The outrage is more than just the location; it is the impropriety of such visible death anywhere. . . . Everything in the world dies, but we only know about it as kind of an abstraction." In her work with death and dying, Elisabeth Kübler-Ross notes that survivors who confront the dead body of the loved one recover more quickly from the loss.

Two recent books offer a direct confrontation with the experience of dying through story and photographs. The first, Mark and Dan Jury's *Gramps: A Man Ages and Dies,* movingly follows the authors' grandfather through the last stages of his life. The other, *To Live Until We Say Good-bye* by Elisabeth Kübler-Ross, follows cancer patients, in pictures and words, through their last days.

EXERCISES ON FEELINGS ABOUT DEATH

Another way to break through our denial of death is to examine death directly. Here are some exercises to help you examine your current ideas, attitudes, beliefs, and feelings about death and dying.

The Words Involved in Death

The words we use or do not use are often indicative of feelings we are comfortable with and feelings that make us uncomfortable.

Words related to death in our society are often euphemisms rather than direct and factual. Try out these words either aloud or in writing. Examine your feelings as you express each word.

Dead	Finished	Murdered
Dying	Passed Away	Abandoned
Gone	Deceased	Grieving
Death	Passed Over	Mourning
Loss	Cremated	
Absent	Buried	

You may wish to add other words to this list. How does each feel? Which are the hardest to say? Which are easy? Which create no particular reaction? Which do you avoid, or wish to avoid? Notice which words are difficult for you, and consider the meaning you give them. You might find yourself remembering something from your past. You might also notice an area of fear. Most important, allow yourself to examine the feelings evoked by this exercise.

To become more familiar and comfortable with words connected with death and dying, use those words in sentences. First note the words that produced anxiety in you in the previous exercise. Now put these words into sentences that might have meaning for you. Write or speak these sentences a number of times and see how you react. For example: My husband is dead. My best friend died. My mother is gone.

This exercise has two purposes. The aim of the first part is to desensitize you to words about death, to help you begin to come to terms with death as a reality and with the concepts that are part of death. The second and more difficult part of this exercise allows you to begin to be more honest with yourself and admit that your loved ones have died or will in fact die. For all of us this is a hard reality with which to grapple. Many of us would simply rather imagine that we will die first, so that we will not have to suffer the pain of loss. Or we deny that

we or our loved ones will die at all. Once we begin to accept
the idea that our loved ones will die, however, we have an opportunity to expand these relationships *now*. When we admit that
there are time limits, we often become more willing to put our
full energy into our relationships, to work through problems,
and to share both positive and negative feelings more fully. We
may also become willing to finish the unfinished business within
our intimate relationships.

Sharing with Another About Death

For many of us, talking about our feelings is a way to clarify
those feelings and understand ourselves better. Also, talking about
death in normal conversation can be very freeing, enabling us
to accept death more fully as a fact of life. Often the other's
sharing or feedback stimulates us in some special way; it can
also help us get closer to knowing and understanding the person
with whom you do this exercise.

Pick a willing friend, colleague, or family member to do this
exercise with you. Each of you will take ten or fifteen minutes
to share your beliefs about and reactions to death. The listener
will speak only to ask for more clarification or detail during that
time, saving personal reactions for his or her turn to speak. You
might be very stimulated by each other's sharing, so it is a good
idea to each take a second turn and share what has come out
during the exercise. You might continue to take five- or ten-
minute turns until your feelings have been fully expressed.

If talking about death in general is difficult, you might relate
to such topics or guideline questions as: What is death like? Burial
or cremation? What should funerals or memorial services be like?
Who has died in your life? What happens after death? Do we
choose to die? Any topic about death that you are both willing
to discuss is fine. You might get ideas from other exercises or
from other chapters in this book.

The sharing process is critical for all of us. It is an opportunity
to examine your own beliefs, feelings, and experiences. Each of

you might learn new ideas, finish with old ideas or experiences, and ultimately gain new growth.

Drawing

Since verbalizing may not be easy or effective for all of us, this nonverbal drawing exercise is included. Drawing can be a means to get to a deeper, less conscious level of knowing ourselves. Like dreaming, drawing may tap our innermost selves, the unconscious part of our minds. Elisabeth Kübler-Ross uses drawing with children who are dying or who have a dying family member. She encourages the child to draw his or her life experience of the moment. She has found that even children who supposedly do not know that a parent is dying give a clear indication in a drawing that they know the truth. Drawing can be an important therapeutic tool for both adults and children.

To do this exercise, arrange to have any size of plain paper and some drawing materials, such as marking pens or colored pencils or crayons, in a variety of colors. No artistic skills are needed to complete this exercise successfully.

Now, start to draw whatever you wish to say about death or dying. You may draw a personal experience, your view of dying or of death, a real or imaginary story about a dying or dead person, or how you experience loss. These are just ideas or guidelines. Draw whatever you feel or whatever comes to mind. Allow yourself enough time to complete your picture or pictures.

After you have finished your picture, study it thoroughly. What do you see? What does it say to you? Any surprise discoveries? What do you learn from your drawing? If you can discuss your drawing with another person, you may be able to bring to light some of your deeper ideas.

EXERCISES FOR FACING YOUR OWN DEATH

Here are some awareness exercises designed to give you an opportunity to look at your own death from a variety of vantage points.

It is hoped that these exercises will enable you to examine some of your beliefs and feelings about your own life and death.

If I Had Six Months to Live

Put yourself in a relaxed position. Now imagine that you have just found out that you have only six more months to live. Consider how you feel. Then ask yourself how you would like to spend the time you have left. With whom would you spend it? What feels important to you now? What feels unimportant?

This exercise is often used by Jim Simkin in Gestalt therapy groups as a means of bringing to awareness what you value or most want for yourself. It is a focusing technique. You may be surprised at what your priorities actually are. Seeing your lifetime as limited, which of course it is, may assist you in creating your life as you truly want it to be. I hope you will implement the ideas you discover from this experiment.

Writing a Will

Make a list of specific items you would like to give to another, after you die. Then ask yourself the following questions:

Was this hard for you to do?
How do you feel about your belongings?
Do they add to your sense of security?
What things are special to you?
What things do you take for granted?
Are you attached to many of your possessions or to just a few?

If you have difficulty sorting out what among your possessions are important to you, try either of these exercises to discover which items you actually value:

1. Imagine you are moving and can take only a few of your belongings with you. Which would you take?
2. If there was a fire in your home, what would you save?

Writing Your Eulogy

Imagine that a eulogy is to be given about you after you die, and you are the writer. Write your view of your life. What are the most important things that can be said about you? What would you say in praise of yourself? What would you omit?

This is another opportunity for you to re-examine your life. Stop and consider what is missing from this eulogy that you would want to be included in the statement about your life. Now is the time to add these missing ingredients, these dreams and desires, to your life.

Death-Fantasy Exercise

The following is a guided imagery experience for gaining perspective on life and death that I learned from Carl and Stephanie Simonton and have used with my clients. You will need to have the instructions read to you while you relax with your eyes closed. You can either put them on a cassette tape ahead of time or you can ask someone to read them to you. The instructions should be read very slowly, to give your imagination time to examine your reactions and ideas.

Sit in a comfortable chair and relax as fully as possible. Imagine a wave of relaxation sweeping over your body from head to toe. Feel each part of your body relax, one part at a time, until your whole body is fully relaxed. Next, lead yourself into a deeper state of relaxation by counting down slowly from twenty to one. Once you are fully relaxed, the journey can begin.

1. When you feel relaxed, imagine that your death is approaching shortly.
2. What are the circumstances of your death? What is the cause? How old are you? What is your reaction to the news or the realization that you are dying?
3. Now see yourself moving toward death. Experience whatever

physical deterioration takes place. Bring into sharp focus all the details of the process of dying. Allow yourself several minutes to experience these feelings and to explore them in detail.

4. See the people around you while you are on your deathbed. Visualize how they will respond to losing you. What are they saying and feeling? Allow yourself ample time to see what is occurring. Imagine the moment of your death.

5. Attend your own funeral or memorial service. Who is there? What are they saying? What are people feeling? Again, allow yourself plenty of time.

6. See yourself dead. What happens to your consciousness? Let your consciousness go off to wherever you believe your consciousness goes after death. Stay there quietly for a few moments and experience that.

7. Then let your consciousness go out into the universe until you are in the presence of whatever you believe to be the source of the universe. While in that presence, review your life in detail. Take your time. What have you done that you are pleased with? What would you have done differently? What resentments did you have and do you still have? (*Note:* Try to review your life and ask yourself these questions no matter what you believe happens to your consciousness after death.)

8. You now have the opportunity to come back to earth in a new body and create a new plan for life. Would you pick the same parents or find new parents? What qualities would they have? Would you have any brothers and sisters? The same ones? What would your life's work be? What is essential for you to accomplish in your new life? What will be important to you in this new life? Think your new prospects over carefully.

9. Appreciate that the process of death and rebirth is continuous in your life. Every time you change your beliefs or feelings you go through a death-and-rebirth process. Now that you

have experienced it in your mind's eye, you are conscious
of this process of death and renewal in your life.

10. Now come back slowly and peacefully to the present and
become fully alert.

This exercise gives you an opportunity to examine your life
and your ideas about death, after-death, and rebirth. It was written "in a way that neither imposes nor presupposes any particular
[religious] faith," but it may enable you to see your own particular
beliefs more clearly. The Simontons noted that the most frequent
reaction to this fantasy was that death was not nearly as frightening or as painful as the participant originally imagined it might
be.

In addition to making death a less frightening phenomenon,
this guided fantasy and the earlier exercises are designed to help
mobilize you or free you to examine, re-evaluate, expand, and
change your life, or some aspect of yourself, right now.

It is interesting to note that the Simontons suggest to their
cancer patients that rather than trying to change unchangeable
family relationships, they might pick new family members *now*
to enhance their lives. Therefore, in imagining we would like a
new mother, for example, we might approach the person who
fits our desired mother image and ask that woman to be our
mother now. This does not negate our already existing relationships, but it does offer a means of expanding relationships and
enhancing our lives. Since sharing this idea with others, I have
added a teenage son and an older brother to my life, two new
and rewarding relationships. Several of my clients have said that
they felt renewed by the idea of "rechoosing" their relationships.
When I recently led a group of eighteen people through this
death fantasy, I was impressed by how many chose to have the
same mother again in a new life.

I hope this chapter has helped you to begin to break through
some of your denial of death. Perhaps you are now willing to

make changes in your life that acknowledge the reality of your impending death and the deaths of those around you.

Arleen Lorrance suggests a way to use our openness to death:

> It would be well for all of us, whether we've been told when or not, to live as if each day were the very last we had. If we did, we'd spend our very precious time doing only what was essential, meaningful, and joyful. We'd never take anyone or anything for granted. We'd invest our energy in rejoicing rather than complaining. We'd quickly take care of any unfinished business and render ourselves up-to-date.

Epilogue

And could you keep your heart in wonder at
the daily miracles in your life, your pain
would not seem less wondrous than your joy.
      —The Prophet

Although the death of a loved one is of course the most overwhelming, any loss or change can be occasion for great pain and distress. I rediscovered this when I completed writing this book, when the seeming end to my creativity began a period of several months that were among the most debilitating I had known in years. Finishing this book was like the death of a loved one for me, for I was bereft without the process and the purpose of writing.

I was startled to find myself so desolate and so uninterested in other aspects of my life. Without the book a sense of loneliness pervaded my days, as if I had lost my best friend, my beloved child, or my lover. I gave myself one month to pull myself together, only to find I didn't feel better in a month. In fact, it was several months before I again became willing to reinvest in my world, to re-establish and create friendships, to return to my psychotherapy practice, even to return to the writing I loved. Grief is like that. And I learned again that grief takes time, its own time, that outside support can enhance the process, and that loss is loss, whatever the loss may be. This is the human experience—and God, it is painful!

Earlier in my life, when I was grieving deeply for my dead brother, I wished there was a book that would help me to understand my internal chaos and to endure the anguish I was suffering.

As I reread this manuscript I realized that out of my earlier suffering I have written the book I had been looking for then.

This is an unusual self-help book about surviving. Since grief is an integral part of the human experience, each of us must face some sorrow, disappointment, and critical ending in our lives. In order to survive we must learn to face loss and grief fully and to trust that we can recover and re-create our lives.

Just as we know that loss is inevitable, we know now that recovering from our sorrow can also be inevitable. We can even use our loss in loving testimonial to the deceased as a step in our own growth, as a positive turning point in our lives.

As we journey through these painful experiences of living, we must never forget that we have an amazing resilience and capacity to survive. Just as whole forests burn to the ground and eventually grow anew, just as spring follows winter, so it is nature's way that through it all, whatever we suffer, we can keep on growing. It takes courage to believe we can survive, that we will grow. It takes courage, too, to live now and not postpone living until some vague tomorrow. If this courage to face life and death can come from reading a book, that is what I wish for each of us.

Appendixes

Appendix A

THE DYING PERSON'S BILL OF RIGHTS

I have the right to be treated as a living
human being until I die.

I have the right to maintain a sense of
hopefulness, however changing its focus
may be.

I have the right to be cared for by those
who can maintain a sense of hopefulness,
however changing this might be.

I have the right to express my feelings
and emotions about my approaching death
in my own way.

I have the right to participate in decisions
concerning my case.

I have the right to expect continuing
medical and nursing attention even though
"cure" goals must be changed to "comfort"
goals.

I have the right not to die alone.

I have the right to be free from pain.

I have the right to have my questions answered
honestly.

I have the right not to be deceived.

I have the right to have help from and for my family in accepting my death.

I have the right to die in peace and dignity.

I have the right to retain my individuality and not be judged for my decisions, which may be contrary to the beliefs of others.

I have the right to discuss and enlarge my religious and/or spiritual experiences, regardless of what they may mean to others.

I have the right to expect that the sanctity of the human body will be respected after death.

I have the right to be cared for by caring, sensitive, knowledgeable people who will attempt to understand my needs and will be able to gain some satisfaction in helping me face my death.*

* Southwestern Michigan Inservice Education Council, quoted in "Ann Landers" syndicated newspaper column, 1978.

Appendix B

THINGS TO BE DONE AFTER A DEATH OCCURS

1. Decide on time and place of funeral or memorial service(s).
2. Make list of immediate family, close friends, and employer or business colleagues. Notify each by phone.
3. If flowers are to be omitted, decide on appropriate memorial to which gifts may be made (as a church, library, school, or some charity).
4. Write obituary. Include age, place of birth, cause of death, occupation, college degrees, memberships held, military service, outstanding work, list of survivors in immediate family. Give time and place of services. Deliver in person, or phone, to newspapers.
5. Notify insurance companies.
6. Arrange for members of family or close friends to take turns answering door or phone, keeping careful record of calls.
7. Arrange appropriate child care.
8. Coordinate the supplying of food for the next days.
9. Consider special needs of the household, as for cleaning, etc., which might be done by friends.
10. Arrange hospitality for visiting relatives and friends.
11. Select pallbearers and notify. (Avoid men with heart or back difficulties, or make them honorary pallbearers.)
12. Notify lawyer and executor.
13. Plan for disposition of flowers after funeral (hospital or rest home?).
14. Prepare list of distant persons to be notified by letter and/

or printed notice, and decide which to send each.

15. Prepare copy for printed notice if one is wanted.

16. Prepare list of persons to receive acknowledgments of flowers, calls, etc. Send appropriate acknowledgments (can be written notes, printed acknowledgments, or some of each).

17. Check carefully all life and casualty insurance and death benefits, including Social Security, credit union, trade union, fraternal, and military. Check also on income for survivors from these sources.

18. Check promptly on all debts and installment payments. Some may carry insurance clauses that will cancel them. If there is to be a delay in meeting payments, consult with creditors and ask for more time before the payments are due.

19. If deceased was living alone, notify utilities and landlord and tell post office where to send mail.*

* From Ernest Morgan, ed., *A Manual of Death Education and Simple Burial* (Burnsville, N.C.: Celo Press, 1977).

Notes

Page

3: The Mourning Period

21   "Mourning and Melancholia": In Sigmund Freud, *Collected Papers*, Vol. 4, p. 152.

23   "pained through": Erich Lindemann, *Beyond Grief*, p. 243.

4: The First Phase of Grief

27   Diane Kennedy Pike: In *Life Is Victorious!*, p. 99.

5: The Middle Phase of Grief

28   Diane Kennedy Pike, *Life Is Victorious!*, p. 102.

29   "Hostile relationships . . .": Erich Lindemann, *Beyond Grief*, p. 243.

36   "When we have something precious . . .": Granger E. Westburg, *Good Grief*, p. 44.

7: Unsuccessful Grief

52   "wooden and formal": Erich Lindemann, *Beyond Grief*, p. 70.

59   In an important psychological study . . . : Ibid., p. 69.

59   "It has been postulated . . .": David Peretz, *Loss and Grief: Psychological Management in Medical Practice* (New York: Columbia University Press, 1970), p. 33.

59   Carl and Stephanie Simonton: In O. Carl Simonton, Stephanie Matthews-Simonton, and James Creighton, *Getting Well Again*.

8: Children's Grief

61   "A child can live through *anything* . . .": Eda LeShan, *Learning to Say Good-by: When a Parent Dies*, p. 3.

64   "Often a child is unable . . .": Violet Oaklander, *Windows to Our Children*, p. 248.

64   Maria Nagy: In her "The Child's Theories Concerning Death," *Journal of Genetic Psychology*, vol. 73 (1948), pp. 3, 27.

67   John Bowlby: In *Attachment and Loss*, Vol. 2: *Separation*.

10: Helping Ourselves with Grief

84   "I needed to set . . .": Diane Kennedy Pike, *Life Is Victorious!*, p. 228.

Page

11: Recovery from Grief

95 "Most people . . .": Frederic Flach, *Choices: Coping Creatively with Personal Change,* p. 78.

102 O. Carl Simonton et al., *Getting Well Again,* pp. 173–84.

13: Loss as a Turning Point

129 "often . . . recall wishing they were dead . . .": O. Carl Simonton et al., *Getting Well Again,* p. 64.

14: Transformation

138 "We are infinitely strong . . .": Albert Rudolph and the Rudrananda Foundation, *Spiritual Cannibalism* (Woodstock, N.Y.: Overlook Press, 1978), p. 5.

139 "At any moment . . .": Viktor Frankl, *Man's Search for Meaning,* p. 191.

140 "I had the feeling . . .": Elisabeth Kübler-Ross, "Death Does Not Exist," a talk given at the Association for Holistic Health in 1976, reprinted in *Holistic Health Handbook* (Berkeley, Cal.: Berkeley Holistic Health Center, And/Or Press, 1978), p. 348.

141 "I personally saw the concentration camps. . . .": Ibid.

142 Peter Koestenbaum: In *Is There an Answer to Death?,* p. 58.

142 *Time* magazine: "Analyzing Jewish Comics," October 2, 1978, p. 76.

142 "ego transcending achievements": Peter Koestenbaum, *Is There an Answer to Death?,* p. 75.

143 "All the hardships . . .": Elisabeth Kübler-Ross, "Death Does Not Exist," loc. cit., p. 349.

15: Breaking Through Our Denial of Death

148 "Therefore give now . . .": Kahlil Gibran, *The Prophet,* p. 21.

150 "It is always a queer shock . . .": Lewis Thomas, *The Lives of a Cell,* p. 113.

155 "Now see yourself . . .": Instructions 3 through 10 are quoted directly from O. Carl Simonton, Stephanie Matthews-Simonton, and James Creighton, *Getting Well Again,* pp. 226–27, with the authors' generous permission.

Page
157 ". . . in a way that neither imposes . . .": Ibid., p. 225.
157 The Simontons noted . . . : Ibid., p. 228.
158 "It would be well . . .": Arleen Lorrance, *Why Me?*, p. 164.

Bibliography

Agee, James. *A Death in the Family.* New York: Avon Books, 1959.

"Analyzing Jewish Comics." *Time,* October 2, 1978.

Antoniak, Helen, Nancy Scott, and Nancy Worcester. *Alone: Emotional, Legal, and Financial Help for the Widowed or Divorced Woman.* Millbrae, Cal.: Les Femmes, 1979.

Becker, Ernest. *The Denial of Death.* New York: The Free Press, 1973.

Bowlby, John. *Attachment and Loss.* Vol. 1: *Attachment;* Vol. 2: *Separation.* New York: Basic Books, 1969.

Caine, Lynn. *Lifelines.* New York: Doubleday, 1977.

————. *Widow.* New York: Macmillan, 1974.

Colgrove, Melba, Harold H. Bloomfield, and Peter McWilliams. *How to Survive the Loss of a Love.* New York: Bantam Books, 1977.

Flach, Frederic. *Choices: Coping Creatively with Personal Change.* Philadelphia: Lippincott, 1977.

Frankl, Viktor E. *The Doctor and the Soul.* New York: Bantam Books, 1967.

————. *Man's Search for Meaning: An Introduction to Logotherapy.* New York: Washington Square Press, 1963.

Freud, Sigmund. *Collected Papers,* Vol. 4. New York: Basic Books, 1959.

Gibran, Kahlil. *The Prophet.* New York: Knopf, 1960.

Gould, Roger L. *Transformations.* New York: Simon & Schuster, 1978.

Grof, Stanislav, and Joan Halifax. *The Human Encounter with Death.* New York: Dutton, 1978.

Grollman, Earl A., ed. *Concerning Death: A Practical Guide for the Living.* Boston: Beacon Press, 1974.

Gunther, John. *Death Be Not Proud.* New York: Harper & Row, 1949.

Hine, Virginia. *Last Letter to the Pebble People.* Santa Cruz, Cal.: Unity Press, 1977.

Jury, Mark and Dan. *Gramps: A Man Ages and Dies.* New York: Grossman, 1975.

Kavanaugh, Robert E. *Facing Death.* New York: Penguin Books, 1974.

Koestenbaum, Peter. *Is There an Answer to Death?* Englewood Cliffs, N.J.: Prentice-Hall, 1976.

Kübler-Ross, Elisabeth. *Death: The Final Stage of Growth.* Englewood Cliffs, N.J.: Prentice-Hall, 1975.

————. *On Death and Dying.* New York: Macmillan, 1969.

————. *To Live Until We Say Good-bye.* Englewood Cliffs, N.J.: Prentice-Hall, 1978.

LeShan, Eda. *Learning to Say Good-by: When a Parent Dies.* New York: Macmillan, 1976.

Lewis, C. S. *A Grief Observed.* New York: Bantam Books, 1963.

Lifton, Robert Jay, and Eric Olson. *Living and Dying.* New York: Bantam Books, 1975.

Lindemann, Erich. *Beyond Grief.* New York: Jason Aronson, 1979.

Lorrance, Arleen. *Why Me?* New York: Rawson Associates, 1977.

Matson, Archie. *Afterlife: Reports from the Threshold of Death.* New York: Harper & Row, 1975.

Moody, Raymond, Jr. *Life After Life.* New York: Bantam Books, 1975.

Morgan, Ernest, ed. *A Manual of Death Education and Simple Burial.* Burnsville, N.C.: Celo Press, 1977.

Morris, Sarah. *Grief and How to Live with It.* New York: Grosset & Dunlap, 1972.

Nagy, Maria. "The Child's Theories Concerning Death." *Journal of Genetic Psychology,* vol. 73 (1948), pp. 3–27.

Oaklander, Violet. *Windows to Our Children: A Gestalt Therapy Approach to Children and Adolescents.* Moab, Utah: Real People Press, 1978.

Pelgrin, Mark. *And a Time to Die.* Wheaton, Ill.: Theosophical Publishing House, 1962.

Peterson, James A. *On Being Alone: A Guide for Widowed Persons.* Pamphlet. NRTA, AARP, AIM, 1909 K Street, N.W., Washington, D.C. 10049.

Phillips, Debora, with Robert Judd. *How to Fall Out of Love.* Boston: Houghton Mifflin, 1978.

Pike, Diane Kennedy. *Life Is Victorious!* New York: Pocket Books, 1977.

————. *Search.* New York: Doubleday, 1969.

Ray, Sondra. *I Deserve Love: How Affirmations Can Guide You to Personal Fulfillment.* Millbrae, Cal.: Les Femmes, 1976.

Rochlin, Gregory. *Griefs and Discontents: The Forces of Change.* Boston: Little, Brown, 1965.

Schoenberg, Bernard, et al., eds. *Anticipatory Grief.* New York: Columbia University Press, 1974.

————. *Loss and Grief: Psychological Management in Medical Practice.* New York: Columbia University Press, 1970.

Simonton, O. Carl, Stephanie Matthews-Simonton, and James Creighton. *Getting Well Again.* Los Angeles: Tarcher, 1978.

Smith, Kathleen. *The Stages of Sorrow.* Totowa, N.J.: Biblio Distribution Centre, 1978.

Temes, Roberta. *Living With An Empty Chair: A Guide Through Grief.* Amherst, Mass.: Mandala, 1977.

Thomas, Lewis. *The Lives of a Cell: Notes of a Biology Watcher.* New York: Bantam Books, 1974.

Wanderer, Zev. *Letting Go.* New York: Warner Books, 1978.

Westberg, Granger E. *Good Grief.* Philadelphia: Fortress Press, 1962.

Wolfenstein, Martha, and Gilbert Kliman, eds. *Children and the Death of a President.* New York: Doubleday, 1965.

ABOUT THE AUTHOR

Judy Tatelbaum grew up in Rochester, New York, received her Bachelor of Science degree from Syracuse University and her Master's degree in Social Work from Simmons College, in Boston.

Grief has been instrumental in her dedicating her life to serving others as a psychotherapist, teacher, writer and friend. A Gestalt therapist with many years experience as an individual and group therapist and supervisor, she worked for several years at Payne Whitney Clinic of New York–Cornell Medical Center, Columbia University School of Social Work, and Massachusetts Mental Health Center before starting a private psychotherapy practice. She resides in Carmel Valley, California. She teaches and leads Gestalt workshops in California, Arizona and Texas, and she is listed in *Who's Who of American Women. The Courage to Grieve* is her first book.

Index